Praise for Peter Thurin

Absolutel

Paul Bassa

Peter has been instrumental in delivering the pride and passion to help achieve our business goals...Totally focused on getting results.

Mitchell Taylor, MD, Taylors Wines

Your high levels of energy and enthusiasm were inspirational to everyone...Thanks again Peter, you are welcome back anytime.

Paul Hitchcock, MD, Goodman Fielder

After our time with **blackbelt in excellence**, I was ready to take on the world...Peter has really changed people...Inspirational, rewarding, energizing—loved it. Outstanding!! Awesome...Peter's positive enthusiastic approach is contagious.

blackbelt in excellence *Conference Delegates*

Guaranteed a greater business future for all of our delegates.

Tony Hasham, Regional Director Asia Pacific, Schwarzkopf Professional

An outstanding contribution

Greg MacDonald, MD, Lloyd Morgan

Lots of fun and immediately relevant to our people...The best we have experienced in 11yrs...challenging and inspiring.

Andrew Moloney, Manager, Flight Centre

The enthusiasm of everything you do is quite infectious.

David Marshall, Manager, Optus

This has changed my whole life...Sensational...I feel great about myself...I can take on the world.

Conference delegates, Sigma Retail Services

Peter is a terrific story teller.
Mike Horton, General Manager, PPG

The benefit of your sessions has been extraordinary…The manner in which you transformed a group of pedestrians into an enthusiastic, energetic and motivated team was phenomenal.
Alex Leombruni, CFO, Club Assist

Best motivational speaker I've seen…How good was Pete!!…This was awesome…Excellent idea…You can take points from this into all aspects of life.
Conference delegates, The Captain's Choice Tour

The experience and the memories was nothing short of brilliant
Peter Fox, CEO, Autobarn

What can I say? How good are you!! I cannot speak too highly of your dynamic and interactive stage presentation **blackbelt in excellence**.
David Williams, Chief Executive, The Leagues Clubs' Association of NSW

Your ability to turn the basics of martial arts into a management tool is uncanny and delivers a powerful message.
Graeme Carroll, CEO, Services Clubs Association

You have certainly entertained, inspired and informed our top performers and achievers in such a way that I'm sure will effect change and so improvement in their lives and work performance.
Warren McCarthy, MD, L.J. Hooker

Nothing but rave responses, Pete. Congratulations on a fantastic job.
Kevin McAulay, Marketing Manager, IGA

I don't think words can explain the effect that Peter had on the delegates and the experience. I do honestly believe it was life changing for many of them.
Director, Wizard National Conference

Your presentation was UNBEATABLE!
Dan Murphy's National Conference

Peter Thurin literally brought the house down with **blackbelt in excellence** and I can't recommend him highly enough. . I will never forget this morning, never, the whole of my life. I feel amazing.
Director, Amgen National Conference

Peter, you continue to deliver a terrific message. Your creative talent and your enthusiasm to the task are amazing.
Wayne Wood, General Manager, Schwarzkopf Professional and Indola - Australia & NZ

Peter was sensational. He blew us away!
David Bennett, Head of Communications - Projects Australia, NAB

Suggestion…..Get TWO Peter Thurin's!
Martin O'Mara, General Manager, National Independent Liquor Wholesalers Association

Since reading Peter's book and participating in his program the sales team are experiencing the best ever results to date. Peter is such an important part of this team & a massive part of our turnaround towards success!
Tim Hicks, State Sales Manager, Taylors Wines

Pete, how fortunate we are to have had the opportunity to work with you and what a difference to our business and culture you have made!
To **be the best you can be** takes a lot of commitment, passion and enthusiasm – and you bring these attributes to life in us.
Barry McGee, Chief Executive, WHK

Peter is clearly your 'not so average' speaker. He got a standing ovation from an appreciative crowd!
General Manager, Bidvest

Truly outstanding!
Manager, McDonald's Australia Limited

Easy to do. Easy not to do.
Your choice!

Best wishes
Peter

be the best you can be

Discover the
small step strategy
to achieve giant
results in your life

Peter R. Thurin

Founder of blackbelt in excellence

Peter Thurin is one of Australia's most sought-after speakers and has worked both internationally and with many of Australia's leading organisations as a compelling catalyst for positive change.

Coming from a successful business background, where he owned and operated several Melbourne pharmacies over twenty years, Peter now speaks on a range of success-oriented topics for a diverse range of companies.

Everything about Peter Thurin and his company *blackbelt in excellence* is dynamic, fun, enthusiastic, engaging, challenging, inspiring, friendly and contagious (amongst other things!). Make no mistake, the call to action is loud and clear!

Peter offers a truly multi-dimensional perspective on achieving success. An outstanding sportsman, Peter twice represented Australia in international tennis and achieved a 3rd Dan blackbelt in taekwondo after taking up martial arts at the age of thirty-six. For many years he has coached junior football and been the chairman of the match committee for one of the country's largest junior Australian Rules football clubs.

Peter is a devoted father and family man. He lives in a suburb of Melbourne with his wife Sharon and their three children Jamie, Melanie and Matthew.

blackbelt in excellence
P O Box 392
Toorak Victoria 3142
Australia
www.blackbeltinexcellence.com.au

First published 2006
Published by *blackbelt in excellence* and Patty Brown
Text design and typesetting by Prowling Tiger Press
Cover design by Digital Evolution
Printed by Trojan Press

National Library of Australia
Cataloguing–in–Publication data:
Thurin, Peter R. (Peter Robert), 1955- .
    Be the best you can be: discover the small step
    strategy to achieve giant results in your life.

    ISBN 0 9757042 1 4.
    1. Achievement motivation. 2. Goal (Psychology).
    I. Title.

    158.1

Part of the proceeds from the sale of this book will be donated to the Australian Council for Children and Youth Organisations (ACCYO).

CONTENTS

INTRODUCTION   1

Who Is This Book For?   3

YOUR CHALLENGE   5

CHAPTER ONE
White Belt: The journey begins!   7

Your Attitude Is Your Choice   9
Let yourself enjoy the simple ecstasy of being
alive and the wonder of the world.   10

It is important to enjoy the journey,
as you move closer to your goal.   11

Your attitude is your choice. You can dwell on
the difficulties or problems, or focus on the
opportunities and solutions. Think about what
you CAN do rather than worrying about
things you can't change.   12

There are very few negatives—no matter
how imposing—that can't be turned into positives.   15

The only limitations are the ones you put on
yourself. And how cool is that? Because you
don't have to put them there! Get rid of them, right now.   16

Don't be a 'gunna' person.   17

White Belt Checklist   20

CHAPTER TWO
Yellow Belt: First Stripe   21

You Need a Sense of Purpose   23
Forget the dictionary for a moment.
'Why' comes before 'How'.   24

Barriers. Sometimes you have to go over the top
of them, sometimes under, sometimes through.
But there are always going to be barriers to
overcome. That's fine.   25

Stop and consider who you are and where you are
in your life, right now, at this moment.   25

As you move towards your goal, be open to different
ways and creative thinking to find solutions to problems.   26

Success must be earned. It does not just happen.   27

If the desire is strong enough, you will work out a way.   27

When it comes to attitude, remember: winners find
a way and losers find an excuse.   28

CHAPTER THREE
Yellow Belt: Second Stripe   31

Time for Action   33
We need to get into the game.   34

Action needs SMART Goals.   35

An achievable, powerful goal is one that is
inspiring, believable and one that you can act upon.   36

Wherever you are, be there.   36

I love the acronym WIN. It stands for What's Important
Now? If what you're doing right now isn't the best use
of your time then why are you doing it? If you are
really serious about doing something, then get
out there and have a crack at it.   37

We need goals, targets, tangible signs of success.   38

We all talk a lot about 'setting goals', but I reckon in
general, we're a whole lot better at setting goals than
we are at achieving them.   39

You need a structure to achieve your goals.   40

It's all about the 'one percenters'.   41

A 'big picture' goal can appear so daunting that
it is difficult to make a start.   42

CHAPTER FOUR
Yellow Belt: Third Stripe 45

Develop and Apply Your Skills 47
It's not enough just to practise.
You must aim for perfect practice. 48

Exams and tests should be embraced.
They give you a chance to show what you've learned. 49

Have you ever considered that the 'best' thing
that can happen is to be marked six out of ten? 50

Life is about going from the bottom to the top to
the bottom to the top and to the bottom and to the
top, over and over again. 51

The only failure is if you walk away, throw it in,
spit the dummy—instead of learning, and then
applying your new knowledge to try again. 52

Optimise your chance to be successful.
Do the preparation. You never know when
opportunity will walk through your door. 53

Yellow Belt Checklist 55

CHAPTER FIVE
Blue Belt: First Stripe 57

Adversity 59
Let's not pretend this will be easy. 59

You can't always be too hard on yourself. Stop, reflect
on your improvement, on how far you've come, and
then re-set goals and focus to keep moving towards
the 'big picture' stuff. 60

How are you going to differentiate yourself?
What have you got—or what can you develop—that
nobody else has got? 61

Tough times require a game plan…or two! 63

We all have certain fears. Of course we do.
We have fear of rejection, fear of failure, fear
that we simply can't do it. Well, you won't do it if
you don't have a crack at it!   64

It's your dream. That's all that matters.   65

Take moments to reflect on the work so far.   66

To achieve your absolute best, you've got to be able
to perform under all conditions.   67

The key is to keep moving.   68

CHAPTER SIX
Blue Belt: Second Stripe   71

The Need to Adapt   73
In life, we need to have the courage to honestly
look at where we are, and what we need to
do to move forward.   74

The definition of 'success' is an ever-changing thing.   75

It's largely the quality of the questions we ask that
will enable us to best benefit from change.   76

Be prepared to think laterally and to engage the
services of people with a different skill set to your own.   77

You cannot do it on your own.   78

Surround yourself with the right people. Those with
the knowledge and the experience that you need,
but also an ability to laugh at you and keep you humble.   80

Let go of people or habits that are holding you back.   81

Great relationships = great family, great friends,
and great business.   82

CHAPTER SEVEN
Blue Belt: Third Stripe   83

Self Image Is Important   85
Your perceptions of yourself, your perceptions of
others and others' perceptions of you can be
powerful influences in your life.   86

Remain humble. 88

Develop your confidence because it will help you
improve. Or should that be: continual improvement
will help your confidence? 89

It's totally fine to look silly occasionally, as long as
you are having a go! 89

Blue Belt Checklist 91

CHAPTER EIGHT
Red Belt: First Stripe 93

Are You Absolutely Committed or Are You Only
Interested? 95
    A warning. 95

We all have 168 hours in the week.
What are your priorities? 96

To do or not to do? That is the question. 97

You must persist. 98

Whatever It Takes. 99

People are not always right. Does it matter
what they say or think? 100

An important note. 101

CHAPTER NINE
Red Belt: Second Stripe 103

C.A.R.E 105
    Care 105

…and while I'm at it, most importantly,
don't forget to CARE about yourself. 106

Have empathy for those around you.
You don't know what is going on in people's
lives, or where they are at. Try to walk in their
shoes, treat them with respect and help where you can. 107

It's okay to be selfish as you begin. It doesn't mean
you don't care. Later, you can give back. 108

CHAPTER TEN
Red Belt: Third Stripe   111

  Do You Walk the Walk?   113
    What DO you value?   114

    The fundamental principles of taekwondo are focus,
    discipline, personal confidence and fun. Wow, aren't they
    so important in all facets of life? And if that's so, shouldn't
    they be the lessons and values we teach to our kids?   115

  Red Belt Checklist   117

CHAPTER ELEVEN
Black Belt   119

  You   121
    There's one thing I didn't tell you about your black belt… 121

    Well, how do YOU feel?   121

Acknowledgements   125

INTRODUCTION

Allow me to introduce myself. Or, to put it another way, who is this guy and why is he writing this book?

Hello. My name is Peter Thurin.

Having completely changed direction in life, today I am a public speaker, business consultant, facilitator, coach and mentor through my company, **blackbelt in excellence**. Before starting this life, I was a pharmacist and a businessman. I have a family—a wonderful wife, two great boys and a beautiful daughter. I love sport and coached junior footy for many years. I have a third dan black belt in taekwondo and I represented Australia at tennis when I was younger. I'm not much of a dancer but I try hard!

So, that's me. What I'd like to say straight away is thank you for buying this book. I'm hoping it turns out to be one of the greatest investments you've ever made.

I'm assuming that you have picked up this book for a reason. Maybe you want to learn guitar. Maybe you have a life-long passion to fly a plane; to speak Italian…in Venice, to own a property or to stop drinking alcohol. That ambition, whatever it is, is your personal black belt and this book has the potential to help you actually achieve that goal.

Notice that I said this book has the 'potential' to do this. Because the book also has other potential. It could act as a door-stop, or a coaster for a hot cup of coffee. Tear out the pages individually and they could be bookmarks for a pulpy crime or romance novel.

But I'm hoping that this book is going to hit a whole different level in terms of usefulness in your life. I'm hoping that it is going to become one of your most cherished personal possessions. It's a lofty wish but if you truly take in what I have to say, and **act on it**, then my claim is not unreasonable.

The key is not the book but **YOU**.

The book is deliberately written in a style that's 'easy' to read. It's a series of anecdotes; of stories along the way. So, you can pick it up and put it down—just make sure you pick it up again! The chapter headings are kind of arbitrary. The stories contain important messages, so take them on board and keep them with you, whether they emerge under white belt or red belt.

Everything I'm going to talk about in the following pages has helped me transform and love my life. I realised at 36 years of age that I had longed to be a black belt in a martial art since I was eight years old. I just hadn't done anything to make that ambition become reality. So I started training. With ageing muscles and a few grey hairs, I got to work. By the time I was 40, I was a black belt and the discoveries I made on that journey have seriously impacted on the rest of my life.

By applying the principles and disciplines of taekwondo to my relationships, my business dealings and every other area of my life, I have made myself more successful in many ways.

I should add that this has not always been easy. It has involved major change and hard work, as well as genuine sacrifices in pursuit of my greater goals.

Importantly, I continue to live and breathe the ideas written about here. They are not esoteric, pie-in-the-sky stuff. They are **easy to do and yet, easy not to do**, practical and most of all, actionable and achievable.

A word you're going to come across a lot over the course of this book is **ACTION**.

Because everything here comes down to **YOU** and everything comes down to **ACTION**.

If **YOU ACT**, you can change your life, you can achieve your ambitions, you can reach your very own black belt. This book can offer advice and guidance. It is a catalyst and a call to action. But only **YOU** can do the actual work.

You've picked up the book, which is the equivalent of the day I went out and bought a brand new, shiny white martial arts suit. It was a significant moment because it showed—for the first time since I was eight—I was now serious about that black belt, that I was taking my first step towards that goal. I committed from that moment to achieving a lifelong dream.

So what is your black belt goal? And how badly do you really want it?

You have invested in this book, so there's your first step. Let's go chase your black belt.

WHO IS THIS BOOK FOR?

Everyone and anyone. I don't care if you're a butcher or a nuclear physicist, a test cricketer or a wannabe musician, a school kid or a grandmother.

We all have dreams and we all have goals. The aim of this book is to help you, in a meaningful, measurable way, to achieve those ambitions.

While I will refer to martial arts and what it has taught me in my own, personal black belt journey, this is not a book about taekwondo or any other martial art. Far from it.

All we need is for you to decide what you want to achieve.

So, what **do** you want to do?

You might want to pass a spelling test, start a new job, improve your health and fitness, overcome being retrenched, make the school team, excel at your existing job, achieve an HD in anatomy, visit the country of your dreams, speak a new language, lose some weight, be promoted, save money, buy a house, be fulfilled in retirement, learn guitar, buy a car, earn a black belt.

The list is endless.

This is not a definitive book on how to live your life. As I have already said, it is a series of anecdotes that hopefully will inspire and challenge you to **be the best you can be**.

Just work out what your personal black belt is because, at that point, we have three vital questions.

- Where are you now?
- Where do you want to be?
- How are you going to get there?

OK, let's get to work.

YOUR CHALLENGE

Before we even start, let's be very clear about the challenge facing you at this moment.

Your challenge is to get something out of this book. Just one thing…hopefully, more than one thing.

And act on it.

It doesn't matter if it's a personal thing, a business thing, or a dream you've had since you were eight, like mine. But do something. Then this book will have had an impact. Don't wait until tomorrow, or think: 'I must get onto that'.

The best time is right now.

CHAPTER 1

The journey begins!

It all starts right here.

Don't look left and don't look right. YOU change your life. You have the control. Take responsibility and do it.

Your Attitude is Your Choice

I wanted to get a black belt when I was eight years old. I finally managed it just before turning forty.

Is this a world record for the longest time to achieve a martial arts black belt? Maybe, but of course the pretty simple reason is that from the age of 8 to 36 years old, I didn't lift a finger towards that goal.

You could spend your whole life wishing you could visit Paris. You could spend decades longing to play the guitar even one-tenth as well as Eric Clapton. You could watch every single Vespa buzz by on the road while ever-yearning that it was you zipping along, feeling the wind on your face and singing the theme song from Roman Holiday.

There's only one reason you don't have that photo of yourself in front of the Eiffel Tower on your fridge, that your friends don't demand song requests from you and your golden guitar fingers every New Year's Eve, that your Vespa is not parked on the footpath outside the café as you're reading this right now.

You.

If you start putting $10 a week aside (any amount is good) then you're taking the first, tiny steps towards France. If you buy a guitar and learn two chords this week, Clapton has every reason to start looking over his shoulder. Have you visited the

Roads and Traffic Authority website to find out what's physically involved in getting your motorbike licence?

These are not massive changes in your life. These are not large demands. But see how you're already on your way? Even these simple steps, on whatever your personal black belt path might be, mean that you've made a very significant mind-shift, from dreaming and wanting to 'doing'. You've embarked on your journey and now I ask you:

How much do you want it?

Will you see it through?

Is this a commitment or just an interest?

For me, at the age of 36, I didn't just keep thinking about a black belt. I went and bought a white martial arts suit, and started my white belt training. The very bottom rung. It took me years of often unbelievably demanding training and discipline. But it all started there, with the purchase of my daggy white suit.

So, what's your equivalent of that suit?

Let yourself enjoy the simple ecstasy of being alive and the wonder of the world.

Modern life can be stressful. The demands on our time and our attention are huge. Work is intense, family demands can be exhausting, and we're bombarded by news and current affairs, advertising and other information at all times.

Sometimes we need to just stand back and strip everything back to basics. The world is amazing and letting yourself see it through fresh, non-jaded eyes can be so refreshing.

I was walking down the street one day when I spotted a woman struggling along with a pram and a little boy, who was maybe two years old. This woman was having a hard time of it because the boy was interested in everything! Every three steps, he was crouching to look at a leaf, or the grass, or a garden gnome in a garden, or maybe a cloud. There was just so much to look at he couldn't look and walk at the same time!

I was laughing at this when the woman reached her goal, a postbox. And if you thought her boy's world was great before, you have never seen such pure, unadulterated joy and excitement as the moment he was lifted up and allowed to insert that envelope into the little slot in the postbox, and let it go.

I don't know about you but I don't often go home at night and say to my family: 'You won't believe it! I did the most fantastic thing today! I posted a letter!' I think that if I did, some people in white coats might show up and suggest that I go with them.

What I saw in that boy at the postbox was that sense of magic in the world. Posting a letter made his day, and why not? When the demands of life get on top of me, I try to remember his attitude—the sheer joy of being alive.

Inspiration is everywhere, all the time and in the most everyday moments.

It is important to enjoy the journey, as you move closer to your goal.

Out behind Melbourne, where I live, there is some beautiful country and one waterfall well worth the walk is Steavenson Falls, near the town of Marysville.

One day, when my oldest boy, Jamie, was only 8 years old, he and I decided to visit the falls. It's a fair hike and we had to do a lot of motivational talking before we left. Was my boy sure he was up for this epic trek? Was he sure his little legs could make it?

OK, what about my ageing pins? Actually, I was pretty confident that I could get there and back…all going well!

Finally, we left the car and began walking, our goal somewhere far, far ahead.

I can't tell you how much fun we had. We laughed and mucked around and hid from one another and giggled all the way there. And the funniest thing is that when we reached our goal, I realised that the falls themselves were the least of the trip—gorgeous though they were. It was the **journey** that made this day live on in my memory. It was my boy and I stepping out together and playing, talking and laughing from the car park to our goal and back again.

We still talk about that day but it's the walk that we both cherish, not how much water happened to be going over the falls on that particular day.

Martial arts taught me a similar lesson. Being handed a black belt three days after I started martial arts would not have meant anything. But by training hard, from white belt to yellow to blue to red and then finally onto black; by putting in the work and watching my skills develop and being surrounded by the people who helped me get there, and who I hopefully helped in return—that was the important thing. Yes, the belt was my symbol of achievement but **it is the ongoing journey that matters.**

Your attitude is your choice. You can dwell on the difficulties or problems, or focus on the opportunities and solutions. Think about what you CAN do rather than worrying about things you can't change.

I used to be a pharmacist. When I started Peter Thurin Village Pharmacy, in the Melbourne suburb of Toorak, there were six pharmacies in the one shopping strip. Of those six, mine was the most likely to fail. (Plenty of people were willing to tell me so when I was thinking about buying it.) Several of the other pharmacies operated with the support of the large chains. Mine was in the worst physical position, with a clearway stopping cars from parking outside at crucial hours of the day. It had been owned by the same popular owner for years and there was a sense that without his presence, it would wither and die quickly. The negatives went on and on—there weren't enough doctors nearby, I had the least floor space of all the pharmacies, my stars were all wrong in that month—you name it.

But my theory was that they were all things I couldn't do anything about. Could I control the fact that the street outside my shop was 'no parking' during peak hour? No. Could I somehow retain the goodwill ghost of the past owner? Nope. Did I want to be part of a giant chain of pharmacies? Not really. That being the case, I had to forget about these negatives.

So I focused on what I could control. I built the best possible team of people, and we worked tirelessly on knowing our products and on remembering every customer's name. Our customer service was a non-negotiable strength—we simply had to be more friendly, more eager, more service-focused than our competitors.

Yes, I sagged a little when I watched supposed friends and acquaintances walk into rival pharmacies on the other, easier side of the street. But could I stop them doing that? No.

What I could do was make such a fuss of them and deliver such spectacular service if and when they did cross my doorstep that it would never occur to them to return to my rivals.

It's all about attitude and recognising that you can influence your world hugely by concentrating on what you can change and where you can star.

I think this is true in life.

Put in the work and enjoy the rewards.

As you may have already gathered, I'm a big believer in putting in the hard work required for success and that true achievements don't come without discipline and toil.

For that reason, I'm also a huge believer in **the importance of celebrating when your hard work pays off.**

Let me tell you about the day I achieved my first grading in taekwondo, moving from white to yellow belt.

Boy, had I done the work. From those early, self-conscious days as the oldest bloke in the training room wearing a white belt, I had worked on my patterns, my punches, my defence moves, everything required of me. I was putting in like no white belt before me.

In martial arts, to achieve a higher belt you must pass a 'grading'. Basically this is a test of your skill which involves set patterns of moves that must be completed perfectly, as well as some combat fighting to show that you can use the moves in action as well as in a set-piece routine.

With heart pounding and as nervous as a kid on his first date, I went through my patterns as a panel of black belt judges watched my every move,

And I can tell you that I passed. I achieved my yellow belt. It was indeed a great moment!

I didn't walk through my front door that night. I kicked it open and burst through, screaming in triumph. As my startled family looked on in astonishment, their 36-year-old father did 'aeroplanes' around the house, running from room to room with a yellow belt fluttering over his head, held aloft in absolute triumph.

And why not? This was a significant moment in my black belt quest—in my personal journey. I had worked and I had achieved. I had toiled and good judges—veteran black belts—had recognised my newly found skills. I was a king! I was the master of my universe! I was a martial arts force to be reckoned with!

It was only recently that I discovered nobody has ever failed that grading!

But hey, so what? I was **now** in the game. I had made a start and I was on my way to 'black'…and beyond!

There are very few negatives—no matter how imposing—that can't be turned into positives.

My boy Matt loves his footy. He's a good player, too; hard at the ball and at the bottom of the packs.

But that can be a dangerous place to be and one day, playing Under-10 footy, he was clobbered in the thick of the action. It turned out he had a broken hand and the doctor was long-faced as he broke the news that Matt was going to be sidelined for eight weeks.

My heart went out to Matt and it was a quiet drive home in the car, his arm freshly plastered. Which is why I was astonished when he turned to me and said: **'Dad, I'm so lucky!'**

'You're what?' I replied.

'I am so lucky. If I'm out for eight weeks, that means I'm going to be ready to play the last game of the season.'

How great is that? Instead of dwelling on the two months in which he couldn't play, when he was forced to watch his team, unable to contribute and unable to do much about his situation, he was looking beyond that—to what he would be able to achieve as soon as that eight weeks was over.

From that day, I have tried to remember Matt's wisdom.

When life kicks us, it's so easy to think about the downside, how fate's been cruel to us, that we didn't deserve this and so on.

Following Matt's thinking, losing a job means there's a whole new opportunity out there, away from that negative place you've been. A relationship breakdown gives you a new chance to find a relationship that works. It's not about a loss of short-term income, or learning to cook for one, not two. It's about the longer-term future and the great days ahead.

Focus on 'what is' rather than 'what if'. Look at what you've got, instead of dwelling on what you haven't.

The only limitations are the ones you put on yourself. And how cool is that? Because you don't have to put them there! Get rid of them, right now.

There was a time when I would have told you that there was no way I could ever hope to go abseiling, because of a lifelong fear of heights.

After a particular *blackbelt in excellence* seminar on the Gold Coast, I was invited by the group to join them for an afternoon of team-bonding rock climbing.

Having preached for an hour on the importance of having a go and trying to **be the best you can be**, I could hardly back away, claiming a fear of heights. So the next thing I knew I was staring up at a very tall wall with an Easy face, an Intermediate face and a Difficult face.

Legs trembling, I started my way up the Easy face and to my relief and joy, I made it to the top. Me being me, I even did a few chin ups at the top to show off!

I was feeling good about my bravery until I watched a fifteen-year-old girl clamber straight up the Difficult wall as though it was a stroll. I was blown away and when she returned I had to ask her: 'How did you do that?'

I expected talk of technique or using certain muscle groups but instead she shrugged and said: **'I just decided I was going to get to the top.'**

She taught me a great lesson that day. Who cares which face of the wall had the easier footholds or hand grips or angle?

I had set my sights too low, deciding that it would be my greatest achievement just to somehow crawl up the easiest face. In fact, anything was possible as long as I made the decision that I was going to get to the top.

And so I did, throwing my fear of heights off the side as I focused on nothing but the top of that Difficult wall. The next thing I knew, I was standing there.

Have a think about your expectations of yourself. Do you ever set your sights too low? Do you believe you're only worth so much money, when in fact there's no reason you couldn't be paid twice that much? Do you think you've done the job after twenty sit-ups when in fact your body could handle fifty, if only you were to *aim* for fifty?

It's something worth contemplating. You set your own limitations in life, so why set them?

Don't be a 'gunna' person.

We all know those people. Are you one of them? Shoulda. Woulda. Coulda…it doesn't count. **Did** you or **didn't** you?

I once caught a taxi on the Gold Coast and, I'm not kidding you, the driver was having real trouble fitting his stomach under or around the steering wheel. We got talking and he volunteered that he would love to go on a bit of an exercise kick to lose weight, but he couldn't find the time.

He had a million reasons why his life was so busy that he simply couldn't even walk or attempt to jog for fifteen or twenty minutes at any point in the day. So his stomach grew. You know the story.

I put a challenge to him. He had told me that he got out of bed each day at 7.30 am, so I got his phone number and told him I was going to ring him at 7.15 am the next day, at which point I expected him to be out of bed and ready to go for that walk. All he had to do was get up fifteen minutes earlier than usual and he could take the first steps, literally, to losing that gut.

He was pumped and we shook hands on it. This was the start of his whole new—thinner—life.

The next day, I phoned him at 7.25 am. A groggy, still-asleep voice mumbled hello.

I said, 'Mate, it's me, Peter, phoning as promised. Where are you?'

'I'm still in bed.'

I said goodbye and hung up. So much for his commitment.

Was I disappointed? Yes, I was—for him. Because I'm quite tough on this point: **you either commit to your goals or you don't.**

It comes down to a few words: Any action is **easy to do, but it's also easy not to do.**

If that taxi driver chose 'easy not to do' then good luck to him, that's his choice. But he will never reach his goal of losing that stomach. He's always 'gunna' do it one day...But not today.

I'm pretty passionate about **'Easy to do. Easy not to do.'** It comes up regularly in my own home.

For example, one of my boys was unfortunate enough to be born with a weedy little body like mine. He recently said to me: 'Dad, I'm thinking of doing push-ups to build up my muscles. If I did 1000 push-ups, right now, would I have a big chest, shoulders and arms?'

I had to explain to him that firstly, if he's never done a push-up, he wouldn't be able to do 1000 straight. Secondly, if he did, he would do some serious damage to his body.

But after we talked for a while, he understood. Upper body strength doesn't come with one spectacular burst of 1000 or 2000 or three trillion push-ups. It comes by doing a few push-ups every day.

At which point, my boy's only challenge is whether he bothers to do the push-ups every day, or not. Easy to do it. But easy not to. It's up to him whether he's **committed** to that bigger upper body or not.

WHITE BELT CHECKLIST

At the end of each colour, we're going to stop, take a deep breath and address a checklist to monitor your progress, assess your feelings about your journey, and think about where to from here. Please take notes because you should revisit these pages, to remind yourself how far you've come and what you've learnt.

- In your personal black belt journey, what skills and knowledge have you **learnt**?
- Which skills or knowledge have you now managed to **apply**?
- Which skills or knowledge have become a **habit** in your life?
- What do you need to do to achieve the next belt?
- Who do you need to help you with this stage of your journey?
- What skills or knowledge can those people bring?
- Do you need more time devoted to your black belt journey at this stage?
- How are you going to schedule this time?
- What's your game plan?
- What's your backup game plan (for when action in the first game plan isn't possible)?
- How do you feel within yourself at this stage of your journey?
- How do you expect to feel if you can achieve your next goal?

CHAPTER 2

YELLOW BELT

First Stripe

Awesome! In martial arts terms, this is your first grading! Congratulations, you're in the game.

You Need a Sense of Purpose

Here's something I know: **If you don't know where you are going, nothing will get you there.**

That's why I've always loved the belt system in martial arts. The belts provide your map. They are a very tangible, logical, easy-to-follow route from a rookie's white belt to a master's black.

All along the way, you get to see your goals coming to fruition, with the big one ever closer. The belts keep you on course and maintain your sense of purpose, which is essential if you're not to lose your way or suffer from failing motivation.

In this chapter, I want to talk a little about motivation and desire, and how they are essential tools in your armoury.

How strong is your sense of purpose?

Often in life I see people who are so close to success but…even in taekwondo, there is a high attrition rate among people who have made it to red belt. The next colour is black, yet they are not prepared to make that level of sacrifice.

The probability of success in anything increases with your willingness to keep going in tough times. It is directly related to your self-discipline in being able to stay focused on your main objective.

Forget the dictionary for a moment. 'Why' comes before 'How'.

Let's start with this book. I've known for a while **WHY** I wanted to write a book. People at seminars would ask if I had a book they could take home to assist them in reflecting on what I'd said, or to offer new things for them to think about.

What I didn't know was **HOW** to write a book. I'd never attempted such a feat before and it's a daunting task—to put so many words together and have it make sense. To turn your spoken stories into prose and to order your thoughts into chapters. I didn't have a clue.

But that was okay, because that was only the 'how' of the project. The desire, or 'why', was strong enough that I was committed to working out the 'how'.

As is often the way, the solution was to find somebody to join my team who did know how to put a book together. So I teamed up with Nick.

And we've achieved a result. The decision-making, the goal-setting, and the discipline to get it done have led to the goal being achieved, resulting in the book you're now holding.

What 'how' means is finding the knowledge, skills, people and disciplines to ensure 'why' is satisfied. 'How' is the bridge between setting a goal and achieving it. The more important thing is to be sure of your goal.

If you have enough reasons 'why', you will work out 'how'.

Barriers. Sometimes you have to go over the top of them, sometimes under, sometimes through. But there are always going to be barriers to overcome. That's fine.

There is no success without adversity. (See Blue Belt, First Stripe)

I've got an athlete friend who was very proud one day because he'd won his very first hurdles race.

Do you know how he did it? He ran in a straight line and knocked over every single hurdle between him and the finish line. He said that nowhere in athletics does it say you have to jump the hurdles; that any of the hurdles must be left standing.

How's that for a way to deal with barriers? I'm not sure it would always work. Sometimes it's smarter to go around, or even over, hurdles than to keep bumping into them.

All that matters is to understand that **there will always be hurdles,** and that this is not something to worry about. Anything worth achieving is going to be difficult: otherwise everybody would do it every day and there would not be the same satisfaction in the achievement.

As long as you don't lose sight of what you set out to achieve, find a way to overcome those hurdles. Life doesn't always give you a clear path, so you have to be careful not to be distracted by obstacles and minor problems along your way.

Stop and consider who you are and where you are in your life, right now, at this moment.

I put it to you that everything you've experienced, everything you have learnt and everything you have done, good or bad, makes you who you are at this point in time.

Obvious stuff I know, but here's the thing: if you seriously consider the impact of that statement, then now is an opportunity to draw a line in the sand of your life.

The past is the past. Draw a line in the sand because where you are NOW and your actions from here, from this moment, will define who you are in the future.

The old saying says you can't change your past. It's right, but you are in control of your future by living to rules you set today and maintaining disciplines that are decided on right now.

It doesn't matter where you were born, or whether you grew up in poverty, or whether you had everything provided on a platter. The rest of your life starts now.

As you move towards your goal, be open to different ways and creative thinking to find solutions to problems.

I read once that a top footballer had learnt ballet as a child. This guy moved as well as anybody I've seen on a football field and I wonder whether it was the unusual preparation of ballet that gave him such great balance and poise? There's every chance.

I know that while training for my higher belts in taekwondo, I decided that I wasn't as good with my boxing skills as I thought I needed to be. I engaged the services of a former world champion kickboxer who later became a contender for a world title as a boxer. Traditional taekwondo training couldn't solve my problem, but that outside influence took me to a different level with my boxing skills.

Ballet for football, boxing for taekwondo. Musicians take influences from everywhere and chefs borrow from other cultures and techniques to improve their food. Don't be afraid to be lateral in your thinking as you chase your black belt. As long as you **don't take your eyes off the main goal**.

Success must be earned. It does not just happen.

blackbelt in excellence did not arrive fully-formed, on a stage, in front of sometimes thousands of people. I did my time speaking to tiny groups of people in back rooms, encountering the suspicious scowls and folded arms that said these people had never heard of me and had better things to be doing with their time. I didn't mind. It only made it all the sweeter when the same people would stay to chat after the session and I knew my messages had somehow got past the barriers and actually touched them.

At a seminar for a major real estate company recently, I was astonished when a woman approached me afterwards and asked if I would consider being a life coach for her, to help her improve in her career and as a person. The thing was, this woman was already the leading salesperson for that company and had a loyal, happy team working for her. But she was still **tireless in her efforts to improve**, to be the best she could be. Far from feeling she had made it, she had her sleeves rolled up and was ready to work harder. I was very impressed...and flattered.

If the desire is strong enough, you will work out a way.

In my early days of coaching junior footy, I invited a leading AFL footballer down to our junior footy club. He told our boys of how he would sleep with a footy almost every night when he was growing up. Many players advise kids to carry a footy with them at all times, bouncing it, handballing into the air, just getting a feel for the leather—but this was the first time a Sherrin had made it to the bedroom, at least in my experience.

For me, I wanted a black belt. I had to face the fact that I had a family, with three kids, and that I had a very demanding business. Yet I had committed to achieving my black belt. It meant that on top of working seven days a week at the pharmacy, despite standing all day, regardless of the fact that I wouldn't let myself drop the number of hours I dedicated to being with my family, I still had to find a way to train up to the level expected of an elite martial arts athlete.

In the end, the only option was to endure 4.00 am training sessions with a black belt friend, Andy, in my garage. It was a crazy, hectic period in my life and often I didn't know how to get from one day to the next, but that was all secondary. I wanted that belt. The rest was detail.

All of which leads to some pretty basic but essential questions for you—questions that will keep echoing throughout your journey:

How badly do you want your goal?

Are you prepared to commit?

Will you sacrifice and be tireless in your quest?

Will you find a way?

When it comes to attitude, remember: winners find a way and losers find an excuse.

I discovered this almost by accident. In my pharmacy, I was determined to stock a particular prestigious cosmetic brand. The problem was that the Company didn't seem to care if I stocked their products or not.

I would phone the sales department in the company's Sydney head office every three months to ask for an appointment with one of their sales representatives. I'd make the call and they'd say no, they had my suburb covered, thanks anyway.

So three months later, I'd phone again and we'd have the same conversation.

After FIVE AND THREE QUARTER YEARS, it was a bit of a standing joke. 'Oh hi, Peter. It's been three months has it? Good to talk to you but no, we're not interested. Talk again next quarter. Ha ha.'

Now, at this stage, you could say I was being pigheaded and wasting all our time, or that I simply hadn't thought to try and change my approach. As I said, it was an accident in the end that answered my question.

I was about to close up for the night when I realised I hadn't made the call to the Company. It was in my diary, as it always was at those three-monthly intervals, but now it was 7.30 pm, not lunchtime when I had always phoned.

I shrugged and thought: 'why not?' So I called and a different voice answered the phone. The only person left in the office that late on a Friday was the Managing Director and he'd picked up the phone!

When I told him who I was and admitted to the past six years of badgering his staff, he almost cried laughing. He could barely speak, he was chuckling so hard. It sounded kind of stupid, I had to admit.

But he promised me a sales rep would be at my pharmacy on Monday morning, and sure enough, I finally got to stock their products. And all because I rang at a different time, after six long years.

I think the lesson here is that **you are never out of options to solve a problem**. Sometimes we have to go to Game Plan B—and don't take six years to decide that, as I did!

Think about the resources available to you now, whether they be people, questions you haven't asked yet, extra knowledge required, more discipline, sheer persistence…just **don't give up**.

CHAPTER 3

YELLOW BELT

Second Stripe

You're working hard but may still be feeling uncomfortable.

Habits don't become familiar overnight, so this is very normal.

Hey, I never said your journey was going to be easy!

Time for Action!

A funny thing about my black belt journey is that the day I passed my grading and actually achieved my black belt is not the memory that sticks most in my mind.

Instead, that memory is of me becoming quite emotional sitting on the end of a weights bench, a week before the grading!

It's true. I was less than a week from the grading and I had just completed a weights session. When you're born with a puny body like mine, you need to do a lot of weights to get up to black belt standards of strength and fitness and I'd never shirked this.

So, on this day, I was sitting on the end of the weights bench, recovering, when it hit me. Everything hit me.

It was as though I could suddenly remember in that one moment, all the hard work. The sacrifices, the support from family and training partners, the endless patterns practice, the hour upon hour of kicking and punching drills, of blocks and other basic moves. I remembered staggering off to the pharmacy after 4 am training sessions, then leaving the pharmacy, bone tired, to train again in the evening. The injuries that I'd endured and the doubts that had been overcome. The list went on.

The tears welled in my eyes. I was about to achieve my goal. I was about to become a black belt.

Muhammad Ali used to say that all the work is done long before you step in the ring and get to dance under those lights. In this moment, I understood. I had no doubt that I was going to achieve my black belt, because **I knew I had done the work. I knew I was ready.**

And that was a great feeling.

So this chapter is about **'action'**. This is about actually making 'it' happen. Because while we all spend a lot of time talking about Vision, Passion, Goals, Ideas and Dreams, the fact is that none of them are worth five cents unless we take ACTION to achieve them.

We need to get into the game.

Often this can be the most important thing. It's easy to put on your gym gear and head off for a work-out but...isn't it also easy not to, for whatever is the chosen excuse of the day?

Easy to do. Easy not to do. Your choice.

For this reason, I say the first and most important thing is to get out there. 'Perfect practice', and other lessons in how to achieve your best, come later.

For now, get into the game.

Imagine a person who decides that to get fit, they are going to run with a friend, 'Mary', each morning at 6 am. What happens when Mary doesn't show up at 6 am? Does our person go back to bed, or does he or she hit the pavement anyway? Mary might be missing out on a great run in front of a beautiful sunrise. Her fault. Her loss.

If we wait for somebody to come along and motivate us,

then the problem arises of what occurs when that person doesn't turn up. Yes, you need a bigger game plan for yourself than hanging around waiting for someone else.

So, throw all that out and self-motivate. If Mary wants to join you on your morning run, fantastic. You'd love the company. But you're out there, whether she is or not…and you're on your way to fitness, regardless of anybody else's alarm clock.

Make a start and the rest will follow.

Action needs SMART Goals.

To act effectively, we need to give ourselves a realistic and achievable goal. It also needs to be very specific. As many of you know, these are what are known as **SMART** goals.

SMART stands for:

Specific
Measurable
Achievable
Relevant
Time Framed

In real terms, that means that while you may set a long-term goal of 'getting fit', you need **SMART** goals to actually get you there.

On day one, it can be as simple and specific as performing two sit-ups, two push-ups and walking to the letter-box and back. But get out there and do it.

Just by undertaking that minor physical activity, **you are letting yourself know that you are serious about this longer-term goal**. A walk around the block will turn into a jog, which will turn into a run. One block will become two and so on.

You just need to get started. You need to get into the game.

In the same way, you might set a grand long-term goal of one day playing guitar at Wembley Stadium in front of 100,000 people. OK, it's an ambitious goal, but why not? To get there, you need a SMART goal on day one. How about a phone call to organise your first guitar lesson? That's not so difficult, is it?

Wembley, here you come.

An achievable, powerful goal is one that is inspiring, believable and one that you can act upon.

As an example, this might be a good goal for a 45-year-old: I want to run a marathon at the age of fifty.

It's an inspiring goal. At the half-century mark, you plan to run 42 kilometres, one of the greatest tests of human endurance, for the very first time!

Yet it's believable. People complete marathons. It's doable. Why not?

And here's the kicker: you can act on it, right now, by putting on your running shoes and hitting the pavement. You don't have to run the marathon today. Just run around the block! What you are demonstrating to yourself is that you have begun the work required to eventually make it across that finish line.

The good news is that you can choose the size of the block!

Think about your personal black belt goal. Is it inspiring, achievable and begging for action right now? If so, fantastic.

Wherever you are, be there.

This applies to whatever you are doing at any given time.

When you are at work, be there. When you are with your family, be there. When you are hitting a tennis ball, be there.

Don't be thinking you should be somewhere else.

I find it difficult to understand people when they talk on their mobile phones while their kids are playing in front of them, aching for them to put down the phone and join in. Who really misses out? Yes, it's the kids *and* the parent, both.

I believe strongly that to achieve the best results, you need to concentrate on what you are doing, right now. If you're at taekwondo training, then throw yourself, body and mind, into that training. The same for guitar lessons, cooking the evening meal and definitely any conversation you engage in.

Don't finish an hour-long lesson or session and realise you were only tuned in for 20 minutes. That's a 20-minute session, dragged out. **Focus, and you'll get to your goals faster.**

I love the acronym WIN. It stands for What's Important Now? If what you're doing right now isn't the best use of your time then why are you doing it? If you are really serious about doing something, then get out there and have a crack at it.

I had this hammered home to me in the pharmacy. At any given time I could have three people asking for new prescriptions, another four wanting refills, two needing advice, somebody lurching through the door with a gaping hole in their leg, Mrs Whoever wanting to tell me how her grandchild went in the weekend's tennis tournament, and somebody's child choosing that exact moment to redecorate the front of the shop with every lipstick tester in the place. This is while both phones are ringing and I've been on my feet for six straight hours.

At that moment, you need to be able to make the decision: What's important now?

Everybody wants your attention, everybody thinks they need you more than anybody else. So what do you choose?

In life, this is a good skill to develop. If you spend time at your workplace doing photocopying when you should be making sales calls, then why are you photocopying? Would the world stop if you didn't photocopy? Then hit the phone.

If you're a nurse who dreams of being an actress, then why aren't you in an acting class right now?

If you desperately want to learn how to cook, then why aren't you reading a cook book right now?

And so on.

There's 168 hours in every week and lots of demands. Only you can sort those demands and use every second to its potential.

Have you put any thought into what is important in your life?

What **are** your priorities?

Achieving those priorities has nothing to do with effective time management and everything to do with effective 'you management'.

So ask yourself: What's Important Now?

We need goals, targets, tangible signs of success.

When you have a long-term goal, it's important to have shorter-term objectives that you can celebrate. After so much hard work and so much thankless slog as you tick off the endless one percenters (and don't worry, you'll learn more about these as you keep reading), you need those moments to enjoy a high five and remind yourself that you are getting somewhere.

In a football match, goals are a reason to celebrate as the team chases the greater goal of victory in the match.

One of my favourite parts of my martial arts journey was when I, or one of my training partners, earned a new belt and we celebrated hard. We were all so happy for each other's success.

Set yourself short-term, achievable goals that you can celebrate as you embark on the longer journey.

We all talk a lot about 'setting goals', but I reckon in general, we're a whole lot better at setting goals than we are at achieving them.

Again, start small. Don't set yourself a goal to surf Pipeline in Hawaii if you haven't first built your fitness and skills in smaller, less dangerous waves. If I said to you today that I want you to climb Mount Everest, where would you even start? It's too daunting. But if I asked you to climb a nearby hill…well, it's a much smaller challenge and you're on your way to bigger things.

Achieving your goal is about discipline. Making the 'decision' is setting your goal. It's the 'discipline' to act and keep acting that will enable you to achieve your goal. That's why you need a strong sense of purpose. The 'want' has to be so strong that you will be able to stay the course.

At first, you might need to take small steps, then success might continue until further improvement gets harder and harder. Then you're back to small steps, inching forward. That's fine as long as you keep moving and keep setting goals that are taking you in the right direction. Start small and then celebrate. You're moving forward…

I'll give you an example. Supposing your goal is to have a happy work or home environment. Start with a single compliment, because compliments are funny things—if people feel good about themselves, they tend to pass that along. If you consistently dish out compliments, you'll be amazed at how achievable your happy environment can be. Small steps, one compliment at a time—yes, one percenters—add up.

Small, easily defined goals help the bigger picture.

You need a structure to achieve your goals.

A lot of that last point, in regard to setting achievable goals and moving forward, relates to having the correct structure for your journey.

Look at this book, a recent goal of mine. I couldn't just start throwing words on pages, or write rambling anecdotes in the hope that it would turn into a book.

I needed chapter headings, and a spine to the book, in terms of what I was trying to say and when. Suddenly, once we got that right, the book had a shape and it was much easier to start filling in the various sections with the most relevant story or argument. (I hope you agree!)

This is one of the clearest teachings of martial arts, where the belt system is the tangible way (structure) of seeing your goals come to fruition. White leads to yellow which leads to blue which leads to red which leads to black. Tennis courts have lines. A structure. It would be an interesting game if we tried to score points without them!

Without structure, your best efforts will be a mess. You need to know where you're going and why.

It's all about the 'one percenters'.

Whether in real estate, tennis, martial arts, banking, you name it—look for ways that you can differentiate yourself from everybody else out there, also trying to do what you are trying to do.

OK, here's a story you might not believe, but it's true. A regular game at the end of a working day at my pharmacy was for the team to demand I empty my pockets. When I did, forty or more small pieces of paper would fall to the floor. We would all roll around laughing.

These papers all held interesting facts about customers from the day's business. If Mrs Jones told me that her son had a big maths test on next Thursday, I scrawled that down as she left the shop. If Mr Smith said he was going away to the coast for the weekend, I wrote that down as well.

The wrong side of midnight would often find me sitting up in bed going through those bits of paper and writing the notes down in a notebook.

Why? So that next time Mr Smith walked in, I could ask, without blinking, how his weekend away went. Was the beach great?

It meant Mrs Jones received a phone call on the Friday, asking how her son's test went.

Why would those people ever think about going to any other pharmacy? Who else would show such a genuine interest in their lives? Such customer service was a huge reason we survived as six pharmacies in one strip turned into two. **We focused on the one percenters. All of us.**

People think I have a fantastic memory. They think I'm brilliant at recalling names or details. In fact, my memory is only average but those one percenters—those bits of paper that we all laughed about—they were what made the difference.

I trained myself to remember such details and it paid off in spades.

Now it's your turn. Think of four or five things that are important in your life. Now I want you to do all of them one per cent better. Then, once that's a habit, another one per cent better again...all these one percenters make a significant difference to your life! I'm not talking about a 100 per cent improvement, a doubling of performance. Just one per cent at a time. **Continual improvement.**

Are you serious...or not?

A 'big picture' goal can appear so daunting that it is difficult to make a start.

We all have self-doubts at different times. That's okay, but don't sell yourself short, in terms of what you are capable of. Have a crack at daunting challenges. You have nothing to lose and, boy, imagine if you **did** happen to pull it off!

Remember, **you can't do everything—but you can do something**. So get started. How many times do we look back and think, 'Hey, that wasn't nearly as tough as I thought it would be!'

Look at the areas of your life that are important. These might include:

Health
Family
Work
Leisure time
Spiritual nourishment

What are your non-negotiables in each of these areas?

Have you even thought about it?

If yes, is your behaviour 'everyday' behaviour? (After all, we're talking about non-negotiables).

If no, there is no better time to start than now. It's time you considered your absolute bottom-line, everyday values or needs in each of those areas.

Just by working out your non-negotiables, you're taking action. You'll have a plan to move forward because you know what you need and want to achieve in each of those areas.

Wow, this big-picture stuff is so much simpler if we just break it down into bite-sized chunks.

CHAPTER 4

Yellow Belt

Third Stripe

The top of your first tree! This is huge, as you prepare to move up to a new colour—a tangible sign of your growth and success.

You're the best of the yellow belts, which means you have already felt the thrill of achievement and you are developing skills.

Develop and Apply Your Skills

Excellence is about consistency. It's about doing the 'good stuff' over and over until it becomes a habit. It doesn't sound as glamorous as sheer genius winning the day, but even sheer genius needs hard work to shine.

Make excellence a habit. Make it the 'norm' and you will be successful. That means developing and then applying your skills.

Success in life is closely linked to three words: Learn. Apply. Habit.

Let's not shirk this: I'm talking about **Behavioural Changes.** This will not be easy but it is the absolute key to achieving your black belt.

In fact, it goes straight back to taekwondo for me. Martial arts is based around the theory of Learn. Apply. Habit.

It works like this: you learn a new punch or kick or even a pattern of moves.

Having practised the new lesson, over and over and over again, you then take it into combat training, because now you need to apply it under pressure. What you are aiming for is the day when you have imprinted the new move into your skill-set so thoroughly that you use it without thinking. It's just there, within you, instead of being a conscious, applied move. At that point, the lesson has become a habit and you can move on to new lessons, new applications.

Tennis players, golfers and other sportspeople use the same kind of training to learn and then refine their strokeplay. Roger Federer doesn't have to think about where his racquet head is on the forehand backswing, and you can bet Tiger Woods doesn't want to be second-guessing his putting action when trying to sink a putt to win the US Masters.

The actual mechanics of their strokes are habit, thanks to the original lessons and then **hours and hours of application**.

You can use Learn. Apply. Habit. in all areas of your life.

If you want to improve your posture, it can take months to stop having to remind yourself to sit up straight—eventually your body just does it without you having to think about it.

If you want to save money, it takes conscious effort to put the money aside each week, or to resist drawing on it to pay some bill or another. After months, you don't even think about the temptation to use the money. Putting it aside, for a greater purpose, is a habit.

It's not enough just to practise. You must aim for perfect practice.

As a youngster, I was a good enough tennis player to make an Australian team and I found myself training under a former Australian Davis Cup player, Colin Long. I thought I had a pretty good serve and I used to enjoy training, where I would hammer my serve to an opponent's backhand or forehand.

Colin put a stop to that. Instead, he placed several tin cans at various points on the service court and asked me to hit the cans with my serve. Suddenly, instead of just aiming generally left or right with my serve, I was trying to target an area that measured only a few square centimetres.

Hour after hour, I aimed at the cans and the ping of a direct hit took a while to become a regular sound. What he had taught me was to **practise with the same level of precision and intensity that I needed in a match.**

If you are sloppy in your chord changes in guitar practice, they won't be sharp when you try to play in front of an audience. If you don't try to get your mouth around the exact pronunciation of the Japanese words you are learning, then how can you get it right when you're in Tokyo, attempting to talk to the locals?

Practise perfect practice. Aim for perfection **every time**, not just when you think you need it.

Exams and tests should be embraced. They give you a chance to show what you've learned.

Most of us hate exams, don't we? It's easy to be spooked by the pressure to perform and the fear that the exam will somehow worm its way into the only areas you haven't learnt thoroughly.

I no longer see tests in the same way. I see them as a chance to showcase the things you have learnt, and the skills and knowledge you possess. It's like a job interview. Do the preparation, as best you can, before you are face to face with the interviewer. In a sales call, again: do the preparation before the time comes to execute the call.

In martial arts, the grading for a new belt or stripe is a big moment and I always looked forward to them. It was my chance to show all the habits I had developed since the last grading. **I had done the work** and applied new skills to the point where

I knew I had given myself every chance to pass the grading.

It doesn't matter if you're facing a spelling test, a dance routine, a maths exam, a driving test or a scuba diving grading. If you've done the work, if you've been honest and tireless in your preparation, you have nothing to fear. In fact, you can show off on the big stage.

And by the way, it's okay to have butterflies before your 'exam'. It's a sign that you take pride in your performance. It doesn't matter how many times I perform on stage, those butterflies are always present while I'm being introduced. Once I begin, I'm fine.

Remember to keep asking yourself: how can I apply this lesson—just like all the lessons in this book—to my specific situation?

Have you ever considered that the 'best' thing that can happen is to be marked six out of ten?

Am I kidding? Six out of ten is the perfect excuse to go and find a dog to kick, right? Well, I'm not so sure—and the dog is very sure.

An average mark hurts at the time but only if you're not prepared to look hard and frankly at where you're at.

What a 6/10 usually means is that you're okay, but it also means that you have to spend more time on your skills, and there's no way around that. You need to know that truth to move forward.

I like to think that a 6/10 can be turned into a 7/10. And from there, an 8/10 is achievable. All of which puts you within striking range of 10/10 if you put in the necessary work.

Marks like 'good', 'excellent', 'poor' give you indications of where you are. They enable you to improve. If you are serious about achieving your goal, you will **embrace such feedback**, not be derailed by it. You'll **find a way to get better**, to be good enough, and then to be excellent.

Remember too that it is better to focus on your strengths. It's easier to turn a 6/10 or a 7/10 into a 9/10 or 10/10. It's much harder to turn a 2/10 into a perfect score. Look at what you're good at and look at the reality. **Be honest and then act. Now.**

Life is about going from the bottom to the top to the bottom to the top and to the bottom and to the top, over and over again.

In martial arts, you start with a white belt, the very lowest belt in the chain. You make your way to yellow belt and suddenly you're at the bottom rung of yellow, trying to earn a stripe. Finally, after three stripes and at the top of yellow, you go for a blue belt grading, and now you're at the bottom of blue belt. Sure, if you look back, you're a long way advanced from those white belt days, but it feels like you're the rookie all over again, with a shiny, barely creased blue belt around your waist.

This is another example of how martial arts mirrors life.

In life, you are led into your first day of kindergarten as the smallest kid in the education system. Just when you have a grip on kinder, and feel right at home there, you find yourself in prep, the lowest level of the primary school system. By year six, you're king of your primary school and, yep, suddenly you're the smallest fish in the much bigger secondary school ecosystem. By year twelve, you're top of the heap again and bang—you're at university, or you enter the workforce, wondering where the toilets are.

Once again, I would ask you to not only accept this truth,

but embrace it. Each time you find yourself at the bottom of a new level, it means you have graduated from the last level. You have moved forward and now there are whole new rooms of knowledge available to you. Your journey can continue and you can edge your way back up the ladder.

There are always fresh opportunities to develop and apply new skills.

The only failure is if you walk away, throw it in, spit the dummy—instead of learning, and then applying your new knowledge to try again.

At many seminars, I ask members of the audience to come to the stage and break some boards with me. You might have seen me do it.

Often, a person will not break the board on their first try. It usually means that instead of hitting the centre of the board with the correct part of their hand, they've managed instead to drive their palm into my fingers, holding the edges of the board. I'm never crazy about this!

The next moment is important, though. I explain to them why the board didn't break and they line up for another attempt. If they hit my fingers again, they haven't processed the lesson that hitting my fingers on the board's edge didn't work last time, that they need to hit the centre and follow through to succeed.

It's a simple example of how to succeed in your broader life. If you try something and it doesn't work, you have not failed.

All that's happened is that you have not yet found the right way to be successful.

My first attempt at owning a pharmacy was in a partnership, and let's just say it didn't go well. I ended up limping out of there with less money than I went in with. As I was mentally licking my wounds, my father asked if I would mind if he rang my former business partner to thank him.

I thought Dad had gone crazy, but later I realised he was right. My ex-partner had taught me some important lessons that I could not have gained from any text book. It was only through this ordinary experience that I realised you can't trust everyone. I now knew I had to learn to negotiate better, to not be afraid to ask for help, to judge people more carefully, to look at myself and ask how I could have done things better, or at least differently. I had to **spend time on honest self-assessment**: I knew I had to improve my life skills.

Lessons learnt from that failed partnership meant that my future success became far more probable. And if my next attempt, Peter Thurin Village Pharmacy, had also not worked, then I would have had to learn more, and try again.

To be clear: the only true failure is if you give up and stop trying. We are continually learning. As you develop your newly acquired life skills, keep applying them to new situations.

Optimise your chance to be successful. Do the preparation. You never know when opportunity will walk through your door.

When I decided to be a public speaker, I spent an entire year hustling around, trying to make companies believe enough to book me for presentations. I spoke to all the right people and I did all the right things.

Do you know what landed me my first paying job? A boozy dinner.

I found myself sitting next to the director of a major real estate company and he liked the sound of what I was planning.

He asked me if I thought I was ready to come in and talk to their sales staff? 'Of course I am,' I replied. Boom. I had a job.

To be totally honest, I'd have to say I was terrified leading up to that first presentation. Maybe the truth is that I had done the next best thing to being totally prepared for opportunity— I had *appeared* to be prepared!

But I did it. In fact, I got up in front of a room full of powerful individuals. Confident, successful real estate agents who had a lot of work to do and looked unimpressed as their boss introduced some motivational speaker, Peter Thurin, who they had never heard of.

He told them that I had run a chain of pharmacies and I could see them universally thinking: 'Big deal. We all run our own businesses within the wider company. And probably make a lot more money than this guy ever did.'

The boss told them that I had represented Australia in tennis. Again, I could almost hear them all think: 'So what? We can all hit a tennis ball if we have to.'

Then the boss said I had decided to get a black belt in martial arts at the age of 36 and was now a highly qualified taekwondo expert. (His words, not mine!)

Now they sat up straight. So when I took the stage the first thing I did was point out that, yes, I was dangerous, and if they didn't give me their full attention I would belt the daylights out of them!

I was joking but I had noticed that it was the combination of martial arts plus business talk that had my audience hooked. Right there and then, I realised this was my point of differentiation and **blackbelt in excellence** was born.

YELLOW BELT CHECKLIST

As before, please make notes on the following questions. Consider the issues they raise and compare your answers—and where you're at now—to the White Belt Checklist. Hopefully, you'll see progress in your journey.

- In your personal black belt journey, what skills and knowledge have you **learnt** since the last Checklist?
- Which skills or knowledge from the last chapter have you now managed to **apply**?
- Which skills or knowledge from the last chapter have become a **habit** in your life?
- What do you need to do to achieve the next belt?
- How are you going to approach this?
- Who do you need to help you with this stage of your journey?
- What skills or knowledge can those people bring?
- Do you need more time devoted to your black belt journey at this stage?
- How are you going to schedule this time?
- What's your game plan?
- What's your backup game plan (for when action in the first game plan isn't possible)?
- How do you feel within yourself at this stage of your journey?
- How do you expect to feel if you can achieve your next goal?

CHAPTER 5

BLUE BELT

First Stripe

Wow. Feel the power of a new belt!

I was standing on a table in a pub as that blue belt was placed around my waist, and blue felt like a whole new world.

My uniform looked different, and I felt like I had taken giant steps. Blue on white looked so much better than yellow on white. I was bursting with excitement.

ADVERSITY

Let's not pretend this will be easy.

I was six weeks away from my grading for a second dan black belt when I broke my hand, badly. To this day, I have a plate and four pins holding that hand together.

It was a disaster. I had been training like a madman, getting myself ready for that grading, a huge goal for me, and now my right hand was literally shattered.

I could have thrown in the towel, right there. I already had a black belt—technically I had achieved my personal goal. The **problem** for me (besides the obvious pain and inconvenience) was that, when it came to martial arts fighting, my right hand was stronger than my left.

And there was my **solution**. Instead of despairing, I found the **opportunity** to develop my weaker left-hand skills. Six weeks later, in the intensity of the grading, I was much more adept at blocking, sparring, and using my left hand for attack and defence. My once-stronger right hand was used as a backup, as required.

If you want your goal badly enough—as I wanted that second dan—**you won't give up. If you don't want it that much, then you may well quit.**

I accepted long ago that you cannot have success without adversity. You simply have to make the non-negotiable decision that no matter what obstacles or roadblocks confront you, you must always search for new solutions.

Yes, in times of adversity, your commitment to your goals will be tested, but that's what makes it so great when you succeed.

You can't always be too hard on yourself. Stop, reflect on your improvement, on how far you've come, and then re-set goals and focus to keep moving towards the 'big picture' stuff.

As a youngster, Jamie, one of my boys, played competitive tennis and there was one match he wasn't looking forward to. The last time he'd found himself up against this particular opponent, in a single-set match, he was beaten six to love. Sure, my son was thirteen years old, compared to the other kid's seventeen years, but he still didn't enjoy getting thrashed.

Heading into this match, we chatted about setting some achievable goals, rather than getting all caught up in winning or losing the match. Jamie decided that the initial target should be to win one game. Let's aim for a score of six to one.

I was so happy for him and proud of him as he won that all-important single game straight away and guess what? With the release of pressure of having achieved that goal, Jamie was able to start going for his shots.

He ended up losing the set, six to four.

This might sound tough, given that the match was never really about winning or losing and we're talking about a thirteen-year-old, but here's the thing, maybe we set our sights too low? The truth is that at four games all, Jamie had every chance to win the set. So while his relief and happiness at having achieved an 'honourable' scoreline was understandable, I couldn't help but wonder what would have happened if he'd had the time and poise to reset his initial goals along the way.

Having won his one game, as hoped for, he was able to play with freedom, as though every game won after that was a bonus.

It would have been terrific had he been able to think to himself when the set was tied at four games all: 'I'm every bit as good as this kid and I'm re-setting my goal, as of now, to win the next two games.'

Of course, hindsight is a wonderful thing and the fact remains that he had achieved a great deal that day, but there was a lesson there in being flexible in your goal-setting. And let's not forget, he was still so young.

If and when you achieve an important goal, then celebrate by all means. **Feel the satisfaction of achievement. But then re-focus and set new, tougher goals for the next part of the journey**. Don't wallow in satisfaction too long. Remember the longer journey you're on, and the bigger overall goals.

How are you going to differentiate yourself? What have you got—or what can you develop—that nobody else has got?

When I made the major life decision to sell my successful pharmacies and attempt to become a public speaker, it was an exciting, yet terrifying time in my life—and not just because my wife was clearly going to kill me for throwing away a perfectly legitimate and secure source of income if my new venture wasn't successful!

The intensity I felt from this major life decision made a formidable backdrop for my first meeting with a speaking agency.

I was right on top of my game—full of energy and enthusiasm. The boss of the agency was friendly and polite and everything I hoped he would be.

Until he leaned back in his chair and said something along the lines of: 'Peter, we have 10,000 speakers on our books. Of those, about twenty get all the work. So get lost, get yourself known and then come back when you've got something to sell.'

I couldn't believe it. Luckily, I had another hard-to-get meeting lined up with the other major public speaking agency. This man smiled sweetly and told me: 'You know, some people are full of energy and present fantastically when I meet them but then totally freeze on stage, while others only come alive on stage. There's no way I can know, from an initial meeting. So get lost and prove you can do it before you come back.'

I could have hung my head. I could have been spooked right there.

But there's an important lesson here: **Listen. Decide. Act**.

What had those two people actually said to me? The core message from both of them was exactly what I needed to hear: 'It's a tough business you're getting into, Peter. This is not going to be a cruise.'

I also realised the first guy had told me I had to stand out from 10,000 other speakers. What did I have? My black belt, the lessons it contained and the on-stage interactivity of breaking boards. Plus I had twenty years' experience of owning my own businesses, and my life was in balance—something a lot of company executives struggle to achieve. I had a wife and three great kids, had played tennis for Australia and I was a coach and administrator of junior football. I was starting to think in terms of my points of difference, and I was also realising that I had to be able to add value.

I made the decision to continue and to prove that I could live in this competitive world. Twenty speakers get all the work? Well, one of them would have to give up their seat, or find another chair for me as No. 21, because I had decided to pursue this.

Then came action. In the wake of those meetings, I spoke anywhere and everywhere. I delivered my presentations in tiny rooms at the back of factories with six people squeezed in to listen. I took every opportunity to hone my presentation.

So when faced with negativity, don't be discouraged.

Instead, **Listen. Decide. Act.**

Tough times require a game plan...or two!

I'm a big believer in having a game plan. In my martial arts training, it was crucial. Anybody who went out, swinging aimlessly, was dead meat. You needed to have a plan of attack and be prepared to fight in a disciplined, thought-out manner to have a chance of success.

But even that was often not enough. I might find myself fighting a taller opponent, or a shorter guy, or an opponent who was an expert kick, or somebody who had lethal punching power.

My game plan had to be changing all the time—often midfight. If Plan A wasn't working, I had to move onto Plan B and maybe Plan C or D very quickly, or my head was in danger of leaving my body.

Well, not quite, but you get what I mean. It's good training for life. As you chase your goal, have not one game plan but several, in case your first plan of attack doesn't beat whatever obstacle is facing you.

Also, remind yourself that just because something is hard, that doesn't make it impossible. People change professions, including me from pharmacy to **blackbelt in excellence**. People move countries, people flee hostile regimes, people are forced to leave relationships. All of these things are hard but they can be done. Your challenges are achievable, so go and confront them.

Again, don't confuse 'difficult' with 'impossible'.

We all have certain fears. Of course we do. We have fear of rejection, fear of failure, fear that we simply can't do it. Well, you won't do it if you don't have a crack at it!

You wouldn't be human if you didn't suffer from self-doubts. There are times when we feel so overwhelmed with everything going on in our lives that we can become stifled, afraid to move in any direction.

Step one is to have a go. I'm constantly inspired by the courage of those prepared to stand up, come on stage and have a go at breaking a wooden board at my **blackbelt in excellence** seminars.

The people in the audience who dare to put up their hand and take a step into the unknown, sometimes in front of a group of workmates who are relishing the chance to take the 'mickey' out of them if they fail (even though these same workmates didn't have the courage to put their hand up and give it a shot). Having said that, usually the audiences are supportive but apprehensive, hoping their workmates will be successful.

And yes, they are successful, and it's always a treasured moment to watch them walk off the stage in triumph, usually with two half-boards ready to be framed.

Do they always break the boards on their first attempt? No. Sometimes people find ways that don't work, but then they try again, armed with that new knowledge, and succeed.

That's what you need to do, whatever your personal black belt journey might be. Be ready to fall on your face for the greater good of having had a genuine crack. And then watch as the next time you succeed. Does it matter if you don't enjoy success every time, first time? **By being prepared to put yourself on the line, you will achieve so much.**

And just as surely, if you don't take those risks, you will not achieve much at all.

It's your dream. That's all that matters.

You know what? There will always be detractors in your life. It's a fact of life. But you and I are not going to let negativity sway us from our goal, are we?

I realised one day that I'd been putting up with these people for years. You know who they are in your own life. Mine were the ones who frowned, scowled and said: 'You're going to start chasing a black belt now? At 36 years old? Why don't you act your age, Peter?' I felt like saying "What do you want me to do? Take up knitting?'

I went and got my black belt.

These were the same people who scowled and frowned when I announced I planned to buy the Toorak Village pharmacy. 'Are you crazy?' they said, before listing all the possible reasons why it wouldn't work and why I could potentially fail.

As I have said earlier, I chose to look at my strengths and what I could control in the business. It thrived, so then the same people scowled all over again, when I announced I planned to sell up and establish *blackbelt in excellence*. 'Are you nuts?' they said. 'The pharmacies are a fantastic business. This new speaking thing will never work.'

Happily, by now I had stopped listening. Such negative commentators on your life are not helpful. All that matters is that YOU believe in your dream, in the achievability of your black belt.

There's a bottom line here and it is this: WHEN you make your dream a reality—not 'if' but WHEN you do it—will it matter who doubted you?

I can tell you it doesn't. In fact, the achievement only feels sweeter.

Follow your own heart and your own dreams...Oh, and try to encourage others in their black belt quests too.

Take moments to reflect on the work so far.

I love my old belts from martial arts. White, yellow, blue and red, with bits of tape hanging off them, and all battered and frayed and worn.

My martial arts journey also left me with plenty of bruises, strains, sprains, broken toes, fingers and a broken hand. And you know what? I don't mind.

In fact, all these things—the physical hurt and the old belts—are my trophy cabinet. They're the trophies that remind me of how hard I worked and how that toil paid off.

Yes, achieving a black belt was the most physically and mentally demanding thing I have ever done. It was unbelievably tough. But...then I remember the lessons learnt, the knowledge gained, and the friends made along the way. These things more than compensate for the tough times, and the belts are a very tangible reminder.

Whatever your journey is, don't forget to stock your own little trophy cabinet, both in your head and in a quiet corner of your house. **When the journey appears daunting, it can be helpful to reflect on how far you've already come and what you've achieved to get to where you are.**

HOWEVER, let's not spend too long in Nostalgia Central, okay?

The trophies are all fine and good but there are more to collect, so it's time to **re-focus and keep moving.**

What's that saying? Life is not a spectator sport.

To achieve your absolute best, you've got to be able to perform under all conditions.

If we only perform when we feel great, on top of life, and the sun is shining, we don't get a lot done. Persistence is a key.

This is where we come down to one of the *blackbelt in excellence* core questions: **are you absolutely 'committed'**? (Refer to Red Belt, First Stripe)

In the months leading up to my black belt grading, 4.00 am starts were the norm. My black belt friend, Andy, would come to my home, we'd back the cars out of the garage and devote several hours to intense combat training before we would both join my family for breakfast. I'd head into the pharmacy by 8.00 am.

But I can assure you that doesn't mean I always bounced out of bed. I wasn't grinning broadly, ear to ear, as I opened the garage door to the man who would try to beat me up before the sun rose. Plus, I was paying him to inflict pain on me. Go figure. Often I was still sooo tired, unable to believe the alarm had just gone off in the darkness. Sometimes I was still in pain from the previous days' training.

But the point here is: **I always got out of bed**. Not once did I tell Andy to go home, that I couldn't be bothered; that just this once, I would skip training. Not once, I promise.

It's the difference between Interested and Committed. Was I committed to achieving that black belt? You bet I was and the 4.00 am sessions were important whether I was feeling on top of the world, or not.

I'll say it again, **if you want it badly enough, you won't give up. If you don't, you will.**

So ask yourself those simple questions: are you prepared to make the sacrifice? Only 'interested'? Or totally 'committed'?

If you answered correctly, you'll go get 'em, sunshine or rain.

The key is to keep moving.

Believe it or not, for all the literature, speakers and other sources of inspiration devoted to the question of how people can achieve success, I think it comes down to this:

One Percenters x Time = Long-term achievements.

That's it. That's how you achieve your black belt goal, whatever it is.

How simple is that? Not one giant step for man, no grand gestures. Just a lot of small steps over time, that combine to equal a much bigger achievement over a long period.

In taekwondo combat, you learn very quickly that if you don't move your head, it gets thumped. Pretty quickly, your head keeps moving at all times, whether you're setting up an attack, or waiting to defend. Your head never stops in the one place because you may as well attach a sign saying 'Hit me'.

Rock climbers also know this truth. If you freeze on a rock, with weight on your legs and maybe one arm, as you search for the next perch, your muscles can quickly turn to jelly. The key is to keep moving, keep distributing the weight so your muscles can adjust, rest, and prepare for the next load.

In the wider scheme, I'm talking about setting goals, working towards them, resetting goals, always doing something to chip away at your grand goal, even if you're not always directly heading there.

If you plan to run a marathon and strain a leg muscle, do you stop your training or do you start swimming to keep your aerobic capacity up? Can you ride a bike without further straining the leg? It's not ideal and, yes, your training has been hampered, but you're still doing something.

There was a time when I would run every morning. Now, thanks to the various aches and pains that taekwondo was kind enough to give me, I still exercise every day but it's not always running. Okay, so now when I run, I carry a sign that says 'I used to be much better than this!'

How can this be specifically applied to your own black belt journey? Easy. Work out a few one percenters—small steps— that you can and will achieve each day. If you do it this way, you will find that it won't interfere too heavily with everything else going on in your life. But also, very importantly, you will be continually improving. (Refer back to 'It's all about the one percenters' in Yellow Belt, Second Stripe.)

I joked about this with a woman who told me she wanted to learn Italian but felt daunted by a whole new language. We agreed that she would learn three words a day—forget learning the entire language, just three words a day was all I wanted. One after breakfast and maybe one before lunch. That's a heavy workload! I suggested she take the whole afternoon off after such a busy morning, learning two whole words! Then learn another one before bed and that's her three words.

Now multiply that by five days a week, times four weeks per month…you can see that before she knows it, she's going to suddenly realise she now knows a fair chunk of the Italian vocabulary.

- Small steps. Always moving.
- Do you need a degree in nuclear physics? No.
- Is it easy to do? Yes!
- Is it easy not to do? Yes!
- It's your decision.

CHAPTER 6

BLUE BELT

Second Stripe

You may still be feeling uncomfortable but look back over your shoulder at when you were a white and yellow belt to reinforce how far you've come.

Maintain your discipline, and keep at those one percenters.

You're heading in the right direction.

THE NEED TO ADAPT

Life involves change. What do they say? Nothing is certain, except death and taxes. To reach your black belt goal, it is not about merely **coping** with change, but rather **embracing** and **benefiting** from change.

Please read that sentence again, because there is a big difference. To cope with change is not necessarily to move forward. You want to do more than that. You need to *use* change to become better.

Change brings new opportunities and allows you to look at your goal from fresh angles and with new eyes. Surrounding yourself with quality people can be an effective way of being ready for change and being able to draw on resources as required. You're going to use change for the better. Our focus is always on continual improvement.

In my life, I am getting better at embracing change, learning from it and growing.

In my working life, I moved from a disappointing partnership to build my own successful pharmacies.

In taekwondo, I used the occasion of my broken right hand to vastly develop my left-hand skills.

I reflect on my parents and grandparents leaving Europe under the shadow of Hitler, to create a brilliant new life in Australia.

You must make the call: direct change so that it works **for** you, instead of coping with whatever change happens **to** you.

It all comes back to the truth that **you can control what you can confront. If you can't confront something, it is likely to control you.**

In life, we need to have the courage to honestly look at where we are, and what we need to do to move forward.

I met a recently retired AFL star at a conference. We got talking and he revealed that he was thinking of breaking up his business partnership. He listed all sorts of problems and the reasons why the business wasn't working and they all came back to this other partner.

Having said all that, he was nervous about calling the meeting to announce his plans to dissolve the partnership.

Not knowing the full story, I said that the only question I would ask is whether the ex-player was satisfied he had done everything he could to make the partnership work before he hit the 'nuke button'?

A few months later, I saw the same ex-player at another conference and asked him if the business partnership had ended, as he'd thought. It turns out it hadn't.

'Peter,' he said. 'I thought about it after we spoke. What I came back to was that maybe I hadn't been doing everything I could. I realised that I couldn't change my business partner, but I could change 'me'.

'I started addressing some of the issues my partner had raised and the problems he had earmarked.'

Guess what. Things were better. The partnership was flourishing and the ex-player was feeling more confident and capable as a businessman. It had only happened because he had the inner strength and courage to honestly look at his own performance. It had been *his* attitude, not the partner's abilities that had been holding them back.

Have the courage and be honest enough to look at yourself and where YOU may need to change in order to move forward.

The definition of 'success' is an ever-changing thing.

Change can happen very quickly, as I like to demonstrate with an example that I often use in my seminars.

Imagine that you are standing on a lonely, deserted railway station platform late at night. As you wait for the train, you might be reflecting on your definition of success.

It might be that owning a fabulous sportscar is your ultimate measure of success.

Or having great kids, or a brilliant relationship with your partner.

It might be that you measure success in terms of how much money you're worth, or how many properties you own, or how many world-class paintings you have created. Success means a different thing for everybody.

But suddenly, out of the mist, looms a large, threatening figure and before you know it, a man has both hands around your throat and is trying to strangle you to death.

Stop for a moment—mid-throttle—and reappraise your definition of success, as against thirty seconds ago.

I'm betting that you now define success as surviving this

situation. The fancy car, homes, money and paintings can go in the river. Even the healthy relationship with family members has momentarily become secondary (although often people say that was a spur to make them act in such situations)—because you are now concentrating entirely on survival. That is now success, for you. To remain alive.

The moral of all this? Don't be too attached to one definition of success. As you chase your goal, other versions of success, other measures of triumph will emerge. Be open to them, both everyday small wins, and massive life-changing victories. **If your focus is too narrow you could miss other opportunities.**

It's largely the quality of the questions we ask that will enable us to best benefit from change.

I can remember the arrival of computers in the pharmacy game. I rolled my eyes. What is this big clunky thing that they want to dump in my already crowded pharmacy, and that they want me to learn to tap and tap and tap all sorts of fine detail into? Do they have any idea how busy I am and how little time I have for such a toy?

Imagine if you still held that view. In fact, how many industries or areas of our lives now genuinely don't use computers? I'm struggling to think of any.

What I should have been doing back then was rubbing my hands together and asking questions of the sales people about what this new contraption could do for me and my business. How could the new computerised system save me time and money? What was it capable of?

When change, even dramatic change, enters your life, don't let yourself fall for the automatic override which longs for the status quo, for things to be as they've always been. Take a good look at what's new and explore how it can make your black belt goal more achievable.

And ask the right questions, such as: 'How can this help me improve?'

Make no mistake, **you cannot change what you don't acknowledge**. So we must return to honest self-assessment here:

Where am I now?

Where do I want to be?

What do I need to do/change/improve to get there?

These questions are ongoing.
Keep asking them.

Be prepared to think laterally and to engage the services of people with a different skill set to your own.

The success chain begins with an **idea**. Then comes the **preparation**, and the careful **planning**. But if all of that is not followed by **action**, it won't count for much. It also means you must be prepared to push yourself into new territory.

In my life as a pharmacist, I once found myself talking to a very successful local businessman. We got yarning about the fact that there were six pharmacies in such a small retail area and how tough the competition was.

Without blinking, he said: 'Peter, why don't you just buy all six pharmacies?'

I laughed. I was thinking to myself, listen to this guy! He's filthy rich, money is obviously not an issue for him and he has no concept of my life: busting my backside, seven days a week, desperately trying to keep my one little pharmacy afloat. He thinks I should buy the other five! He's kidding…isn't he?

Not surprisingly, when I snorted and shook my head, he was gone, and probably never gave it another thought.

But how big an idiot was I? As I thought about it later— unfortunately, much later—it occurred to me that this man was very successful for a reason. He obviously knew things about business and about expanding businesses that I could not hope to know in my daily battle to make my pharmacy successful.

I didn't let myself consider his question. I wasn't prepared to step outside the business that I knew to ask him what he meant, how I could do that, what the ramifications would be? Would he even be prepared to work with me to make it happen?

I took the lazy man's way out: my brain went into 'shut down' mode. His idea was just too hard. **The absolute fool-proof excuse for failure is to wait for everything to be perfect before taking action. I confused 'difficult' with 'impossible'** and sat on my hands.

To my detriment…but hey, we all make mistakes. That was one of mine and I've made plenty of others since…but they've been different ones. The trick with mistakes is to learn the lessons they provide.

You cannot do it on your own.

The essence of *blackbelt in excellence* is to **be the best you can be**. Yes, you have to commit, but to be your best, you have to leverage the strengths of others too. Who do you need on your team?

In my martial arts quest, I quickly worked out that I needed all the help I could get. Just as at school, we need teachers, and at university, we need lecturers, I needed great instructors. But I also needed people to train with me one-on-one, such as Andy and our 4.00 am combat sessions in my garage. I needed to talk about my diet with an expert and I needed my family for support and encouragement. (I still do. My wife and three kids are my team in life.)

Since starting **blackbelt in excellence**, I have had the great pleasure of consulting to many big businesses as well as small-to medium-size businesses. You don't have to be Einstein to notice that they all have one thing in common: it takes more than one person doing all the work to make these companies tick. Certainly that was never more true than in my pharmacies, where a carefully selected and nurtured fantastic team carried the day.

The key to this is to offer credit and encouragement to those who are assisting you. Was it enough that I was paying poor Andy to show up at my house at four in the morning for months? No. It was important that I regularly thanked him for his commitment and for his support in my black belt quest. Thanking him was never difficult, by the way. I was endlessly grateful that an established black belt would rise so early to help me. Andy? He just smiled sweetly and said that having the chance to beat me up for a few hours was a great way to start his day. I think he was joking. Then again…

So who is on your team? More importantly, who should you be giving credit to? Whose shoulder should you be putting your arm around? To whom do you need to say 'thank you'?

Surround yourself with the right people. Those with the knowledge and the experience that you need, but also an ability to laugh at you and keep you humble.

As a young tennis player, I was greatly improved by the wisdom and experience of my coach, former Davis Cup player Colin Long. While battling to make my Toorak pharmacy successful, I consulted business mentors for specific questions and rules for success. In martial arts, two names stand out: Bernie Victor and Andrew Rozinszky. (Actually, that's not strictly true. The two names that stand out are Bernie and 'Roy', after a famous incident at Uluru in Central Australia, when we walked off a plane en route to a presentation and found a man holding a greeting sign that indicated he was there to meet Peter Thurin, Bernie Victor and someone called 'Roy Sinky'. We all fell on the tarmac laughing, when we realised that somehow Andrew Rozinszky had been lost in translation. We laughed so much that the people behind that event must have thought they'd hired a bunch of live ones.)

These two have worked with me since the inception of *blackbelt in excellence* and I don't think any two people on the planet have laughed at me more, or kept me more grounded. We have performed in front of thousands of people around Australia and overseas. When I asked Andrew, *aka* Roy, for his all-time favourite memory, he recalled that Uluru presentation, where he and Bernie had thirty minutes to set up boards and martial arts gear for 400 people, all in thick red sand in exhausting heat under a cloudless sky. He remembers intense pressure. I asked him why that was his favourite memory if the conditions were so tough. He replied: 'Because the back drop was Uluru, and because **we made it happen** for 400 people! We did it! **It was magic.**'

Plus, of course, that trip gave him a nickname for life.

Bernie's favourite memory was a trip to Queenstown in New Zealand. He had his wife, Lydia, and daughter, Holly, with him and I'd taken my eldest son, Jamie, so **there was a lot of family bonding**. Plus we were at a fantastic venue and presenting to a very excitable audience from the USA. In fact, it's the only time I've ever been given an enduring standing ovation **before** starting the presentation. Don't you just love the Americans?

The point is that these two have been right with me for years, the three of us **laughing and joking and supporting one another** at every step. They are wonderful guys with great skills. Working with quality people is a powerful way to move to higher levels of performance and to **be the best you can be**.

Let go of people or habits that are holding you back.

For *blackbelt in excellence* to work, I needed people who believed in it, and in me. I needed people with complementary skill sets—like the speaking agencies who would market my concept to seminars and conferences, or like Nick, who helped me write this book, or Stuie, who put my website together and, by the way, was my training partner when we attained both our second and third dan black belts.

They're people who are on my side and helping me grow.

By contrast, the 'wrong crowd' will only hold you back, either by acting in ways that clash with your new resolve (do you really want to party until 3.00 am if your goal demands you're up at 6.00?) or through their negativity. They will only squash your ambitions. (Refer to 'It's your dream. That's all that matters' in Blue Belt, First Stripe)

It sounds harsh, but when you move on from those people, you are free to achieve your best.

Great relationships = great family, great friends, and great business.

This is the happy flipside to that last point.

My small, boutique, wrong-side-of-the-street pharmacy boasted the Number One pharmacy account for Christian Dior in Australia for one reason: we had a great relationship with the Christian Dior team. They looked after my team and my team looked after my customers, happily enthusing about the great Christian Dior products. It made sense to me and—guess what—it worked.

The martial arts component of ***blackbelt in excellence*** would be a shadow of itself if I wasn't backed by Andy and Bernie, looking our audience in the eye, encouraging them and teaching them their skills.

This, for me, is possibly the most exciting part of life—the simple fact that **once you find your team**, once the mix of skills and personalities 'clicks', **you take off.**

From there, anything is possible. Plus you've got great people to share it with!

What could be better than that?

But underlining it all remains my family. Have a great relationship with your family and everything else flows from that.

CHAPTER 7

BLUE BELT

Third Stripe

Congratulations. You are now over halfway.

Think about what that means.

By now, you are not content to just 'get it done'.

By now, you should be a little tougher on yourself, aiming for 'perfect practice'—to perform your new skills and disciplines every time, and perform them well.

SELF IMAGE IS IMPORTANT

How you see yourself, and the confidence you have in yourself, is vital for peak performance. **You must believe in your ability to achieve your goals.**

When you're facing a wooden board, perception is everything. The board won't break itself. You have to believe you can put your hand or foot through that wood.

Remember the story of Sammy the horse? A guy's car got bogged out in the country and a farmer brought his only horse to the rescue. He was an old, blind horse that was going to have to pull the car out of the mud all by himself.

The farmer hooked Sammy up to the car and cracked his whip, yelling 'Go Tommy! Pull!' Nothing happened.

Then the farmer cracked the whip and yelled 'Go Harry! Pull!' Still nothing.

Another crack and the farmer yelled 'Go Charlie! Pull!' Nothing.

Until finally the farmer yelled 'Go Sammy! Pull!' and Sammy pulled the car out.

The driver was grateful and thanked the farmer, but asked why the farmer had yelled the other names? The farmer replied: 'I told you Sammy is old and blind. If he'd thought he had to pull the entire car out alone, he never would have attempted it.'

How many challenges do you not take on because your perception is that it's too hard?

What I like about that story is that poor old, blind Sammy **was** capable of pulling the car from the mud—he just didn't know he could do it by himself. Are there times when you look at a challenge and immediately give in to your usual self-doubts? That you're not skilled enough or strong enough or game enough to attempt that challenge?

Yet, when faced with natural disasters or life-threatening situations, we often hear about people performing 'superhuman' feats of strength or courage to save their own, or other people's lives. Good old Sammy the horse dragged an entire car, simply because he had no idea he was attempting it on his own.

Don't sell yourself short. You might be capable of a lot more than you give yourself credit for.

Your perceptions of yourself, your perceptions of others and others' perceptions of you can be powerful influences in your life.

Bernie, of *blackbelt in excellence* fame, worked as a postie for a long time as he threw himself into his martial arts training. When he'd tell people that he was a postie, they'd immediately make all sorts of assumptions about how smart he was (or wasn't) and about his life potential. However, once he had finished competing internationally, Bernie put himself through university and completed a degree in biomedical science. It makes you wonder about how quick we are to judge other people.

Likewise, at a conference in New Zealand, I was very

nervous in the company of a huge Maori man with lots of traditional tattoos and a menacing look about his huge bulk. It turned out he was the loveliest, most gentle man—and had been nervous of me because he knew I was trained in martial arts. How strange that our summation of one another had been so far out.

Or there was Rick, now a long-time friend, who I may or may not have opened the door of my pharmacy to on Christmas Eve years ago. It was after hours and I was sitting on the floor at the front of the pharmacy, literally surrounded by money. I hadn't had the chance to go to the bank because we'd been so busy. All the team, having worked tirelessly on a huge day, had gone home. There was a hammering on the door. This wild-looking guy had parked his ute right outside and was desperate to get into the pharmacy. It occurred to me that he could be a druggie or a thief, but it was Christmas Eve so I opened the door. At this point, the guy, Rick, reached into his pants...and pulled out a huge wad of cash.

It turned out Rick hadn't done any Christmas shopping and this was his one and only chance. He practically bought out every expensive perfume or cream in the shop, stopping every now and then to say: 'Peter, this is costing me a fortune!' Of course, I loved it. But he had no option and became my single biggest customer ever.

If I had judged him on that first impression, I wouldn't have opened the door and an opportunity would have been lost.

Be very careful about being hasty in judging those you meet along your journey. The most unexpected people can have much to offer you and, I hope, much that you can offer in return.

Remain humble.

Exactly one week after I had achieved my black belt, and was feeling pretty good about myself, I participated in a jujitsu seminar for black belts. This was an exclusive weekend for those who had earned a black belt in any martial art. It enabled black belts to fight against one another in a closed environment. Jujitsu is a grappling martial art, as against my discipline of taekwondo, which is a kicking and punching martial art, so I was looking forward to engaging in a different field of combat and—hey, after all, I was a black belt!

With my stiff new belt around my waist, I marched in there and was promptly brought back to Earth. I reckon I 'died' at least three times that weekend. Wow, did I get my butt kicked by the more experienced, more skilled practitioners. And I learnt many valuable lessons—one of which was to stay humble and not get carried away with my achievements.

I'm always humbled by the amazing energy generated in a conference room by people achieving what they weren't sure they could, breaking boards. People are so excited by their achievement and often have us autograph their broken boards so they can frame the pieces. It's heady stuff, but when I get home and tell my kids that I've been signing autographs, they laugh at me and are very quick to tell me to pull my head in!

As you achieve success, don't get big-headed. Appreciate those who have helped you get to where you are, and be aware of how far there is to go.

Humility with success is a wonderful mix.

Develop your confidence because it will help you improve. Or should that be: continual improvement will help your confidence?

As you become better at something, you definitely feel more capable and more confident about applying these new skills. At the same time, it's important to take a moment every now and then to reflect on your improvement and let yourself feel that flush of success.

I see this all the time when I conduct **blackbelt in excellence**'s martial arts-plus-keynote sessions. This is a unique session that we have had enormous pleasure presenting in different places around the world.

Often, conference delegates are only told to wear gym clothes and arrive at the session having no idea what they are about to be subjected to. This group of people, initially right out of their comfort zone, transforms in a two-hour period into a much more confident, powerful, higher-performing team.

It's about having the confidence to attempt something new and then using that experience to develop new skills and continually improving those skills throughout the session.

A very different level of 'confidence' leaves the session.

You need to build confidence to give you momentum for the next steps of the journey.

It's totally fine to look silly occasionally, as long as you are having a go!

How's this for a Hall of Fame embarrassing moment?

One day, while demonstrating board breaking in the early days of **blackbelt in excellence**, I was doing a 'push kick' to break the board. This is probably the easiest technique there is to use in this situation. I was in front of about 200 women—and, sadly for me—my martial arts directors, Andy and Bernie. I was so busy talking and explaining to the group that I did not follow through with my kick, so the board did not break.

My foot made a kind of dull thud as it hit the board and stopped. I can still hear the raucous laughter of Andy and Bernie who have **never** let me forget it. Don't they realise I was trying to demonstrate how **not** to do it?!

At least I was having a go! I look forward to being laughed at by Andy and Bernie for many years to come.

Blue Belt Checklist

It's that time again. Please make notes on the following questions, consider the issues they raise, and compare your answers, and where you are at now, to earlier checklists.

- In your personal black belt journey, what skills and knowledge have you **learnt** since the last Checklist?
- Which skills or knowledge from the last chapter have you now managed to **apply**?
- Which skills or knowledge from the last chapter have become a **habit** in your life?
- What do you need to do to achieve the next belt?
- How are you going to approach this?
- Who do you need to help you with this stage of your journey?
- What skills or knowledge can those people bring?
- Do you need more time devoted to your blackbelt journey at this stage?
- How are you going to schedule this time?
- What's your game plan?
- What's your backup game plan (for when action in the first game plan isn't possible)?
- How do you feel within yourself at this stage of your journey?
- How do you expect to feel if you can achieve your next goal?

CHAPTER 8

RED BELT

First Stripe

It is time to celebrate a new colour.
There's light at the end of the tunnel.
We all know what the next colour belt
is.

But do not relax! There's still a lot to be
done.

Are You Absolutely Committed or Are You Only Interested?

A warning.

I should tell you that in martial arts, the red belt level is where a lot of people fall off their quest for a black belt.

It always surprised me that red belt was where so many people bowed out—and in particular at Red Belt, Third Stripe! The very next belt is black, so why would you stop now? I guess the work required just became too hard, and they didn't have the fire in the belly to see it through. Remember, **it's the difficult times that truly test your commitment to your goal** and the work becomes markedly harder between red and black belts in martial arts. I guess some of these people had wanted to be fit, to be able to defend themselves, whatever their motives were, yet not enough to climb the last, most difficult, yet most rewarding and exciting stage of the mountain.

So be warned: this is where you could shrug and roll over in bed, instead of going for that 6.30 am run as you've promised yourself you would, and as you have up until now.

As always, the answer is in the one percenters. Remember?

The little things. So do **something**. Now! But keep moving—you'll get through this flat spot and suddenly there's the summit, right there.

Close your eyes and picture yourself standing there, arms raised in triumph.

Now, let's go…

We all have 168 hours in the week. What are your priorities?

When I decided to chase a black belt, there were plenty of logistical reasons why I shouldn't, even beyond the simple damning statistic that I was 36 years old, creaking around in an inflexible body and possessing no skills. But worse were the everyday logistics—my 'duties'. I was running the pharmacy, which was literally seven days a week, every day of the year. And I mean every day. Easter, Christmas, New Year's Day. All of them. Plus I had a family.

I was on my feet from 8.00 am until closing time every day. If I was really lucky, I might sneak a sandwich for lunch, standing over the sink out the back between demands for prescriptions or sales reps or all the other things that come at a pharmacist from all sides all day.

I'm not going to kid you that it was easy to drag my sorry butt off to training at the end of such a long day (having already trained before work). It wasn't. But I am proud to say that I never once missed a training session just because I was too tired to go, or because I didn't manage to get myself there.

The fact is that I had made the black belt a priority in my life. Just as my family was and always will be an unswerving, non-negotiable priority, and the success of the pharmacy was a priority, so was my goal—to achieve that belt—whatever it took, and whatever I had to sacrifice to find the extra hours in my week to do it.

There are the same number of hours in your week as there are in mine. You do have time for exercise, for learning that language, for meditating…whatever you think you *don't* have time for. So what are your priorities?

The Lesson: There are 168 hours in everybody's week. What are you going to do with that time? How committed are you? (Refer to Yellow Belt, Second Stripe: What's Important Now?)

An exercise: Monitor how you spend your time for a couple of weeks. Be brutally honest. Look at where you waste time, where you decide not to head out for that run, where you could have gone the extra yard. I think you'll find there are windows of opportunity there to chase your goals.

To do or not to do? That is the question.

I've mentioned this earlier, but it's worth emphasising again here. As you get closer to your ultimate goal, the work can become more demanding and it is here that people often start to shirk the hard work required.

A non-negotiable bottom line for me is that talk is cheap and action is all that matters. You know that by now. You also know that I am not prepared to compromise one centimetre on the belief that **if the 'want' is strong enough, you will. If it's not, you won't.**

As I travel around Australia and overseas, I hear so many **interested** stories. People with dreams and aspirations, but when you drill down, they are not **committed** to these things, which means there is a good chance they will not happen.

After one presentation, I sat down with a salesman who was

away from home a lot and worried that his relationship with his three teenage boys was being damaged by the absences. We came up with a workable game plan to enable him to keep in touch with his boys, and to really use the time he had with them. It was all very achievable and would make a difference. Three years later, I met the same man. There had been no change, but he had lots and lots of excuses as to why he hadn't put our game plan into action.

He wasn't even committed to his relationship with his kids, while claiming his greatest fear was those relationships breaking down.

Our plan would have been so easy for him to execute. As it turned out, it was easier for him not to.

It's time to get back to chasing your goal. There's that same old question: do you want it?

You must persist.

I understand tough times. I really do. I know how hard it can be to stick to your goals.

Rewind to the first year of *blackbelt in excellence*. I had just given up my professional life, where I owned several successful pharmacies with a secure, solid income, and now I was sitting in a small office, concerned that my mobile phone was broken.

The phone looked fine but it hadn't rung for so long that I found myself assuming it must be damaged in some way. On more than one occasion, I actually rang the mobile from my landline to check that it was receiving calls.

The bad news was that the phone was fine. It was just that nobody outside of my office was dialling that number.

Not many people can tell you to the cent what they earned over a twelve month period. I can. From the date of selling my pharmacies, over the next year of establishing **blackbelt in excellence**, my income was exactly zero.

That was a very frightening time and I could easily have succumbed to self-doubts, fear of failure, sagging motivation…all the usual demons that lurk around us.

But I persisted and finally that mobile phone began to get some work. It rang a few times. Then it started to ring a lot.

If you truly want your goal, then you cannot give up. It's that simple.

Whatever It Takes.

Not only can you not give up, but you must be prepared to do whatever it takes—obviously within the borders of reason. I do not condone any actions that are harmful or unethical.

Remember when I phoned the cosmetics company every three months for six years to win that account? Well, so much of what I learned about persistence and the truth of **whatever it takes**, I learned from my daughter, Mel.

When she was six years old, she wanted a dog. I mean, she REALLY wanted a dog! Her whole life revolved around us getting a dog. The only problem was that I was not a big fan of dogs.

She badgered me and badgered me. She argued strongly all the great points about dog ownership. I was immovable in my opposition.

Then one day I went out to check the mailbox and was more than a little surprised to find a letter from God. Written in a surprisingly childish hand for the Almighty, the letter explained to me that it was very important for my daughter to have a dog. The letter was, of course, written by Mel.

Guess what? We ended up with a dog!

Not long afterwards, I was interstate to open a conference for a large global company. There would be 250 delegates and we had been invited to do a martial arts demonstration and I was to deliver a keynote address. It was exciting stuff.

With one minor hiccup. I discovered at 6.00 the night before that the delivered wooden boards were too thick for the delegates to break. In fact, Bruce Lee in his prime would have had trouble breaking these boards even if you gave him a hammer! Would my daughter have cancelled the board-breaking part of the seminar? Not likely. We had to find a Sydney timber mill and do an awful lot of work in a short time. At 2.00 am, the boards were re-delivered, cut to the right thickness. Andy, Bernie and I were red-eyed the next day but the conference was awesome!

We had done whatever it took to make sure that it happened.

How serious are you? Are you prepared to make the sacrifices? Are you Interested, or Committed?

People are not always right. Does it matter what they say or think?

Only if you let it.

Let us consider this list for a moment:

Elvis Presley
Marilyn Monroe
The Beatles
JK Rowling
Peter Thurin

You'd be correct to wonder what on earth I think I'm doing putting my name in among such company. Don't worry, I'm not having delusions of grandeur. In fact, the connection is that everybody on that list suffered rejection.

JK Rowling saw her original Harry Potter manuscript rejected by 17 publishers before one finally spotted the magic within those pages! A record label executive famously told The Beatles, when they were young, that 'all guitar bands are out'. Elvis was fired by a concert manager and advised to return to truck driving. A modelling agency, in showing Marilyn the door, suggested she learn secretarial skills or maybe get married. I had two leading speaking agencies politely tell me to come back when I had something to offer.

Understand, I am not attempting to compare myself to Elvis or any of the others on that list. But I do understand rejection.

People don't always get it right and it really doesn't matter what they say or think.

So my advice, in the face of doubt or criticism, is to seek wise counsel, listen, decide, then act.

If you think the criticism is unwarranted, then follow your path. If you think the criticism might have some merit, take it on board, act accordingly, then follow your path.

Remember, it's the tough times that test your commitment to your goals. Listen, decide and act. As you know, these lessons are ongoing.

An important note.

OK, we've established **you** are committed. That's fantastic.

Now we need to talk about everybody else.

Please understand that as you approach your black belt, people look 'at' you and 'to' you for guidance and inspiration. It is essential that you conduct yourself in a manner that is in keeping with the essence and the spirit of being a black belt.

The last two stripes of Red Belt are devoted to some of the 'softer', yet no less important, principles integral to the belt system.

You will notice also that the following chapters are shorter than those that have preceded them. Do not be fooled. They are, as I have just said, equally important.

This is about synergy. It's about all parts (chapters/lessons) working together to have a far greater impact than any anecdote/stripe/coloured belt on its own.

CHAPTER 9

RED BELT

Second Stripe

At this stage, everybody has an expectation of you—you're almost a black belt but you're facing a mountain of work.

This is the real test of character—it's about having the courage and the perseverance to keep going. This will really test your commitment to your goal; this will really sort out how badly you want a black belt.

This is about attitude. Exciting stuff!

C.A.R.E.

Care

In my world, CARE is an acronym. It stands for:

Customers Are Really Everything.

It also stands for:

Colleagues Are Really Everything.
Children Are Really Everything.
Choices Are Really Everything.

If you embrace this concept of CARE, your course of action is reasonably clear. It becomes important to remember people's names and if you care enough, you will train yourself to get better at this. There are many techniques, such as associating a name with a trigger word, or simply writing names down in a notebook. Sure, we all laughed when I pulled out little bits of paper at the end of a day at the pharmacy but I remembered details that made a big difference to my customers.

Think about what your customers, children, or other important people want from you and hope to receive from you.

I once turned up at a speaking agency at the same time as a

well-known public speaker. As we were both standing in the foyer, I noticed that the receptionist was clearly a big fan of the other speaker. You could just tell that she could barely believe that he was standing there, in real life, right in front of her and she would actually get to meet her hero.

Finally, she worked up the courage to start a conversation, and asked him how he was. Without even looking at her, he reeled off one of his standard lines: 'If I was any fitter, I'd be dangerous.'

And then he was gone, through to her boss's office, leaving the receptionist looking like she might cry.

So much for CARE. There was a guy who had built a huge reputation as a man whose teachings were worth listening to, and he didn't have 30 seconds to genuinely care for somebody who believed in him.

If your child has a story he or she wants to tell you, genuinely listen. If a customer has a problem, apply yourself totally to helping them solve it.

Remember to CARE.

...and while I'm at it, most importantly, don't forget to CARE about yourself.

Have you ever looked at the safety instructions when you board an aeroplane? I am always intrigued by the part where they say if oxygen masks drop out of the roof, make sure you have attached your own before attempting to help children or other people around you.

It sounds selfish doesn't it? Worrying about your own breathing before thinking about your kids. But it actually makes sense. Because if you're breathing poison, or passing out from lack of oxygen, or whatever horrible thing they're worried about, then you can't help anybody else.

The key is to secure your own breathing so you can be more effective in helping others in that crisis.

It's a good lesson to take into your everyday life. **If you're not taking care of yourself, how can you truly care for others?**

So while most of this chapter is about empathy and caring for those around you, don't forget to dedicate the time and energy necessary to ensure you're at peak performance. This will give you the greatest opportunity to have a positive effect on those around you.

Have empathy for those around you. You don't know what is going on in people's lives, or where they are at. Try to walk in their shoes, treat them with respect and help where you can.

At a **blackbelt in excellence** seminar, I once had a 60-year-old lady break a board. Her reaction was astonishing! She gave me a bone-crushing hug and then planted a huge kiss. I can assure you this is not commonplace! There were tears streaming down her cheeks.

Why? It turned out that she had been struggling to find the will to continue living. After 35 years of marriage, her husband had recently left her for a much younger woman. Meanwhile, she had battled some ill-health. Life was tough and she had thought it was all slipping away. I hadn't known any of this as I called her to the stage, nor had I known that for this one lady, breaking that board—when she hadn't remotely believed she would be able to as she began the attempt—would turn out to be a major moment in her life. That board had revived her belief in herself, and in what she might be able to achieve.

Another time, we were packing up, having just finished a conference for an international hair care company. (It was actually the seminar where we'd been up until 2.00 am, making sure the boards were the right thickness, so we were exhausted.)

A woman approached me. She suffered from the disease lupus, along with other ailments that were seriously affecting her physically. Both hands were covered in bandages for a start. She hadn't wanted to ask in front of the entire company but now they were gone, she asked if she could attempt to break a board.

She said she just needed to know—*really* needed to know—if she could.

Well, in the end, there were three big tough black belts, two senior managers from the company and this brave woman, all crying as she broke that board.

I remain humbled to have been present at such a great moment for that lady, and proud that Andy, Bernie and I didn't even hesitate, finished for the day and tired as we were, to have empathy for her request.

It was empathy that gave me one of the greatest moments in *blackbelt in excellence* history.

It's okay to be selfish as you begin. It doesn't mean you don't care. Later, you can give back.

In the early days of my martial arts journey, I sometimes felt uncomfortable because it seemed to me that I was nothing but a 'taker'. I was soaking in lessons and techniques and encouragement from all the martial arts people around me but didn't have much to give back, beyond raw enthusiasm.

It was only with hindsight that I could see this was okay. Once I did have skills and a high belt ranking, I happily joined those offering advice and encouragement to the new group of white and yellow belts, now taking their turn at being selfish.

Keep this in mind for your journey. Don't be too worried by being selfish, by asking for what you need from those around you because, as you progress, the time comes to 'put back in', to teach and encourage and help those who have not yet reached your level. It's all part of embracing the belt system.

It also means that you have a responsibility to do so. Certainly, in martial arts, it is clearly understood that those who have reached the higher belts have a duty to assist the lesser belts.

The good news is that you'll be amazed how fantastic it feels.

This is one of the reasons that I received so much enjoyment from coaching junior footy as well as playing and watching sport over the years. I thrive on the chance to help kids develop their skills, learn to be part of a team and enjoy the thrill of competition. Working with kids is a passion of mine. For those of you who do the same, I am sure you understand what I am talking about.

The circle turns, we help one another as people should, and feel good in doing so.

CHAPTER 10

RED BELT

Third Stripe

This is preparation for show time.

Remember it's a layered journey: yellow plus blue plus red leading ultimately to black.

By now, with very honest, unflinching hard work, you should be ready for black.

If you approach the black belt moment with the attitude of a winner, confident that you have done the work, you can then demonstrate the required skills and expertise to achieve your goal.

DO YOU WALK THE WALK?

The question I'm most often asked at seminars is: 'Do you still train in martial arts?'

It's interesting, isn't it, how people want to know that you are still actually doing what you are talking about.

Once upon a time I had a pharmacist who worked with me in one of my pharmacies. At staff meetings, one of his key messages was that the customer always came first, no matter what. It didn't matter if you were midway through calculating some figures, or stocking shelves. If a customer arrived, they came first. In my opinion that advice was, and still is, spot on.

However, there was one small problem. After a while, the rest of the team started to notice that the rule applied to everybody except the pharmacist himself. If he was the one working on some figures in the dispensary, a customer could wait for hours as far as he was concerned. Whatever he was doing was more important than the customer's needs.

Respect certainly fell away quickly after that. Because this guy was not walking the walk. Talk is cheap.

You can't preach healthy living and then get caught smoking if you expect people to keep listening to you and respect your message. You can't talk about honesty all week and then rob banks on the weekend!

Decide what is important to you and make sure your behaviours reflect that.

What DO you value?

This is not about me. It's about you. So, what are YOUR values?

Have you thought about this? Earlier we talked about the things that you consider to be non-negotiable in major areas of your life, such as family, work, leisure, spiritual matters and so on. But now we're talking about non-negotiables in terms of how you operate as a person.

Ask yourself, and answer honestly, how important to you are values such as respect, integrity, honesty, accountability, excellence, teamwork, strength, and a willingness to see things through?

It's easy to say all the right things on this particular subject. We all know that we're supposed to nod earnestly and talk eloquently about how we consider ourselves to be people of substance and that our word is our bond, and so on.

But I'm asking you to make a very honest self-assessment. Are you truly living according to your values?

I was at a very large corporation's conference in Couran Cove, Queensland. It was late in the night and the second most senior man in the company, who had obviously enjoyed too much red wine, confided: 'Peter, what am I doing here? The company has cut my bonus. I'd rather have the cash in my hand than have to be here conferencing with my people.'

I was amazed. This was a company leader and he was telling me that his core values put his bonus ahead of spending time developing his team and building relationships with his work-mates. Yet I'll bet if I'd asked him, when sober and sitting at his desk, whether that was true, he would have given me a long speech about his integrity, commitment to his people, and so on.

By the way, the topic I was to speak on to open the conference the next day? Yep, 'Building high performing teams'.

So please spend some time to meditate on this. **Are you happy with your core values, AS YOU ACTUALLY LIVE THEM, not as you talk about them?**

The fundamental principles of taekwondo are focus, discipline, personal confidence and fun. Wow, aren't they so important in all facets of life? And if that's so, shouldn't they be the lessons and values we teach to our kids?

If you are a parent, but also if you are in a leadership position, it's important to remember that people follow what we do, as opposed to what we say. At the start of this chapter, I spoke about the pharmacist I worked with who preached customer service but actually had no commitment to it. That's a road towards zero credibility.

It's why I need to be fit, well prepared and confident when I make presentations. If I turned up looking overweight, disorganised and unsure of my message, it would be difficult to inspire people to take charge of their own lives.

It is also why *blackbelt in excellence* sessions are interactive. There is no point in me just talking to people about self-defence or breaking boards. They need to do it for themselves.

If you **tell** somebody something, they will probably forget.

If you **show** somebody something, they may or may not remember.

But if you **involve** people, hands on, in what you are doing, you increase greatly the chances of leaving an impact and lodging the lesson in their memory.

Again, the lesson here is clear. The fundamental principles of taekwondo are a great framework for your life. You need to live them, and involve those around you, if you are to make an impact.

RED BELT CHECKLIST

The same questions (remember, they are 'all the time' questions) but now quite a different feeling as compared to those early days.

- In your personal black belt journey, what skills and knowledge have you **learnt** since the last Checklist?
- Which skills or knowledge from the last chapter have you now managed to **apply**?
- Which skills or knowledge from the last chapter have become a **habit** in your life?
- What do you need to do to achieve the next belt?
- How are you going to approach this?
- Who do you need to help you with this stage of your journey?
- What skills or knowledge can those people bring?
- Do you need more time devoted to your black belt journey at this stage?
- How are you going to schedule this time?
- What's your game plan?
- What's your backup game plan (for when action in the first game plan isn't possible)?
- How do you feel within yourself at this stage of your journey?
- How do you expect to feel if you can achieve your next goal?

CHAPTER 11

BLACK BELT

You've done it. You're a legend.

There's just one thing...did we mention there are other summits to be climbed from here?

You

There's one thing I didn't tell you about your black belt...

Being a black belt is great, but you can be better. It's a brilliant reward for all the work you have done and you have a right to feel very proud.

But you are not yet the best you can be. I am not the best I can be.

It's time again, as we have at every stage through your journey, to redraw the line in the sand and set new goals—to aim for perfection.

How can you apply what you have learnt from this book, or your journey, to your wider life and to other goals?

We must always be focused on continual improvement in all facets of our lives at all times. It sounds tough, but there it is.

Well, how do YOU feel?

It starts with a dream. The bigger the dream, the greater the foundation you need to put it into place and make it real.

Build a boatshed, small foundations.

Build a house, large foundations.

Build a hotel complex, a whole lot bigger again.

You get the picture.

By now you know how to achieve great results. A solid foundation, the preparation, and then action. It's actions that lead to results that give you the opportunity to celebrate.

Your black belt is a celebration.

You have moved through a process.

By now you will have developed great habits (or at least better habits!)

You understand the importance of focus and the constant need to move forward.

Continual improvement with the emphasis on the one-percenters.

A confidence exists that was not evident or felt when you started your journey.

Your self-esteem is well and truly intact.

You have demonstrated that consistent persistence (or is that persistent consistency?) is a key to success.

You have a right to feel proud.

But, keep raising the BAR. (Belief. Action. Results.)

Strive to be a little bit better tomorrow than you were today.

Life is a balancing act, so make sure there is a semblance of balance in your life.

I thought when I started my martial arts training that it was about learning to fight.

Now, as I reflect, I know that I am a different person.

My thinking, my physical well-being and my positive outlook have evolved.

I have enjoyed 'the trip' immensely.

I have had fun.

My black belt has opened up a whole new world for me.

Today, as you know, I travel the world 'talking' and using martial arts, which I started at the age of 36, as a metaphor.

Can you believe that? I get paid to talk! Not bad for a bloke who used to sell jelly-beans and razor blades!

Life is what you make it. Keep challenging yourself.

I congratulate you and hope, one day, to have the opportunity to share stories with you.

be the best you can be.

Best wishes

Peter

ACKNOWLEDGEMENTS

My Wife—Sharon ('Shazza')

CEO of Slim Secrets—world's greatest health bars! Never wanted me to sell my pharmacies but now the Number One advocate for *blackbelt in excellence*. I think she loves the fact that I travel so she has the bed to herself! Lots of laughs in 28 years of marriage. Bring on the next 28!

My Kids—Jamie, Melanie (Mel) and Matthew

My greatest fans and vice versa. They love me (and I definitely love them), they take the "mickey" out of me, they keep me grounded. They allow me to be an integral part of their lives. I am indeed so blessed. Thank You!

My Parents—Gerdy and Ricky

While others doubted, they only ever believed that *blackbelt in excellence* would be incredibly successful. My whole life, they have never stopped believing in me, supporting me and loving me.

My In-Laws—Marlen and Leon

I've always said I couldn't have chosen better in-laws. It makes me smile to know that time has shown me to be correct.

My Entire Extended Family and Friends

While we all do 'our thing', we never stop caring and looking out for each other. Thanks to you all for your encouragement and support.

Andy 'Roy Sinky' Rozinszky and Bernie Victor

The Directors of Martial Arts at *blackbelt in excellence*. They have been with me from the beginning. We've travelled, we've entertained, we've impacted, we've laughed. Long may it continue.

Stuart Cargin
My Martial Arts training partner (2nd & 3rd Dan). My website designer. So often my source of discussion. We've come a long way Stuie!

Nick 'The Terror' Tetoros
A former world champion kick boxer and world ranked boxer who keeps me fit. I think he enjoys hitting me!

Pharmacy Colleagues
To everyone and anyone who ever worked with me in my pharmacies. I'm not sure how you coped but I do know we laughed a lot.

Martial Arts Instructors
Especially Jack and Alf—It is difficult for me to imagine what you must have been thinking when I first started training. Thanks for your patience and persistence.

Patty Brown
My publisher. Great warmth. For some reason, Patty knew where I was coming from at the very beginning.

Anyone who has worked with and inspired kids
The hope is that we have a powerful, positive impact on the kids but the bonus is that it makes you feel great too.

blackbelt in excellence **working with Charities**

There are so many wonderful charities that do so much outstanding work.

I am extremely proud of the contribution that sales of **be the best you can be** have made to so many of these amazing organisations.

Being a father of three children, I have a passion for kids and a leaning towards children's charities. Having said that, *blackbelt in excellence* is absolutely focused on continuing to support worthwhile charities.

If you would like to know more, please contact us through our website: **www.blackbeltinexcellence.com.au**

At **blackbelt in excellence**, we make it a priority to learn about your business and your challenges and to respond to your brief effectively.

The tailored presentations (including the internationally acclaimed Martial Arts + Keynote Workshop) we deliver to your people will be relevant, purposeful and specifically designed to engage and challenge them in exactly the right way to inspire action and achieve results. And yes, you can be successful and have fun along the way!

We understand that every business faces its own unique challenges in achieving success. Your people will walk away with absolute clarity about the steps they need to take to achieve their goals—and your business objectives.

blackbelt in excellence specialises in:

- Conference, seminar and workshop facilitation
- Keynote presentations and on-going programs
- Master of ceremonies
- Performance consulting
- Coaching and mentoring
- Team building through martial arts activities

---

blackbelt in excellence
P O Box 392
Toorak Victoria 3142
Australia
www.blackbeltinexcellence.com.au